CAMPUS SECURITY:
SITUATIONAL CRIME PREVENTION IN HIGH-DENSITY ENVIRONMENTS

by

George F. Rengert

Mark T. Mattson

and

Kristin D. Henderson

Criminal Justice Press
Monsey, NY
2001

Dedications

To Arlene, who took time from her busy career to do my share of the family things while I worked on this book.
George Rengert

To my father-in-law, John Reilly, for a lifetime of friendship and support.
Mark Mattson

To Ginny, my mother and friend, for your never-ending strength, love and encouragement.
Kristin Henderson

ISBN: 1-881798-30-5

CONTENTS

Acknowledgments

We owe a debt of gratitude to Lieutenant Robert Lowell of the Temple University police department, who was a partner in much of this research. He provided the critical police viewpoint that academic types often overlook when we write and talk to each other. We are tempted to say that it never hurts to get the view from the street, but sometimes it does hurt; although it always makes us better analysts. Thanks Bob for a job well done.

We thank the Department of Campus Safety Services at Temple University. Specifically, we thank Vice President of Operations William Bergman. His unwavering support allowed this research to occur. We extend our appreciation to Detective Steven Amrom for all of the assistance he provided throughout the project. We also extend our appreciation to Mr. Robert Keough, whose GIS expertise was invaluable, and Ms. Kelley Klick, without whom the survey administration would not have occurred.

The research reported in Chapters 3 and 4 was conducted under grant #98-IJ-CX-0001 from the National Institute of Justice. Points of view and opinions expressed in this book are ours and neither reflect nor represent the official policies or positions of the National Institute of Justice or the U.S. Government.

LIST OF FIGURES AND TABLES

CHAPTER I.
INTRODUCTION

In recent years, the U.S. public has become alarmed about violent personal crimes on college campuses. Although these crimes are rare, the media have often sensationalized violent offenses on campus, thereby creating a sense that campuses are unsafe environments for students everywhere (Karp, 2001). Concern has increased despite consistent evidence that campuses are safer than the communities in which they are located (Bromley, 1999; Lizotte and Fernandez, 1993).

Perhaps most publicized was the 1985 homicide and rape of a Lehigh University coed, Jeanne Clery, in her campus dormitory (Sloan and Fisher, 1995). This case was instrumental in bringing national attention to security and safety issues on university campuses. The coed's parents, Howard and Beverly Clery, began a national campaign to convince state and the federal governments to pass legislation requiring campus administrators to release information about university security policies and crime statistics. The Pennsylvania Legislature was the first to pass a law requiring, among other things, the publication of campus crime statistics. At least 14 other states have followed this lead (Griffaton, 1995).

Federal lawmakers also responded by passing the Student Right-to-Know and Campus Security Act (1990). This act requires campus administrators to report various crime statistics as well as campus security policies in order to receive federal funding. The original act had several shortcomings: there was no central collection point for campus crime statistics; the crime of larceny/theft was not included; and there was no requirement to include a "population at risk" in the form of student or campus population data (Bromley, 1999). Some of these deficiencies were addressed in the 1998 amendment. For example, the amended act designated the U.S. federal Department of Education as the agency to receive campus crime data (Roach, 2000a).

The Department of Education has only been collecting comparable statistics on campus crime since 1997, and to date has published data for the three years 1997 through 1999 (U.S. Department of Education, 2001). These data are not directly comparable to those published by the Federal Bureau of Investigation in the Uniform Crime Reports since all non-police personnel are required to report criminal incidents on campus (with the exceptions of religious and professional counseling personnel), while only crimes reported to the police are voluntarily reported and recorded in the Uniform Crime Reports. Furthermore, since individuals other than students can be the victims of a crime on the campus of an educational institution, using undergraduate enrollment as a base measure understates the size of post-secondary education institutions (U.S. Department of Education, 2001). Missing are faculty, graduate students, staff members and friends of students, who also may be victimized on campus. This results in campus crime rates being overstated in the Department of Education's statistics.

Nevertheless, it is instructive to compare campus crime rates per 100,000 undergraduate students on campuses with federal rates per 100,000 persons living in the United States. The following statistics on campus and United States crime rates were taken from U.S. Department of Education (2001:5-9). The crime instilling the most fear in the American public is criminal homicide. A total of 11 murders occurred on U.S. campuses in 1999, compared to 24 in 1998 and 18 in 1997. Using simple undergraduate enrollment counts, the rate of criminal homicide at post-secondary education institutions was 0.07 per 100,000 students in 1999. By comparison, in 1999 the homicide rate in the United States was 5.7 per 100,000 persons over all and 14.1 per 100,000 persons ages 17 to 29; the latter more closely matches the age groups on campuses. These figures illustrate that students on college campuses are significantly safer from homicide than residents of the nation as a whole.

The same pattern holds for other crimes. The national rate of sex offenses on campus was 14.8 per 100,000 students, while the rate of rapes alone exceeded 32.7 per 100,000 residents in the United States in 1999. The robbery rate was 12.0 per 100,000 students versus 150.2 per 100,000 persons in the U.S. The aggravated assault rate was 22.6 per 100,000 students versus 336.1 per 100,000 U.S. residents. Finally, the most common crime reported to the Department of Education was burglary. The burglary rate on the campuses was 156 per 100,000 students, compared to 770 per 100,000 inhabitants nationally. Clearly, campuses are much safer than the country as a whole.

Defining Campus Crime

Federal officials were faced with the problem of how to define a campus for crime-reporting purposes. For example, is a building that houses a privately owned fast food restaurant on the first floor and campus offices on the upper floors considered part of the campus? Are public sidewalks alongside campus buildings included in the definition of a campus? In the legal case of Donnell v. California Western School of Law (1988), the California Court of Appeals declined to extend a college's duty of protection to off-campus property even though that property immediately adjoined the campus. The law school occupied an entire city block, and the attack occurred on the public sidewalk that ran along the side of the building (Smith, 1995).

A similar problem is evident at the University of Pennsylvania. The university was accused of "creative bookkeeping" when a map of robberies in 1995 revealed that those counted by university administrators as campus crimes were in similar locations to those counted as off-campus. In fact, campus crimes often were surrounded on either side by crimes counted as off-campus. Kalstein (1999:5) charges that the University of Pennsylvania "has been less than forthcoming when publicizing crime statistics." Other universities have been similarly charged (Kalstein, 1999).

The issue of on- vs. off-campus crime is not as obvious as it might seem. The problem is that many universities own and/or use buildings in the neighborhoods surrounding the campus. If a robbery occurs on the sidewalk beside one of these off-campus buildings owned and/or used by the university, it is not clear whether or not it should be recorded as a "campus crime." The courts have clearly held that the sidewalks are not on campus if they surround the campus but are not within it (Donnell v. California Western School of Law, 1988). Therefore, spatial clusters of crime in and around these buildings may include both on- and off-campus crimes. A crime counted as on-campus may have occurred *within* the building owned and/or used by the university; others in the cluster may have occurred on the sidewalk in front of or across the street from the building. In most cases we do not even know whether the victims were students, university employees or neighborhood residents. Thus, it is not yet clear how to define a campus that does not have a distinct boundary.

Federal officials continue to struggle to develop a common definition of the campus boundary, and to regulate how campus and community officials apply this definition. In the 1998 amendment to the Campus Security Act of 1990, Congress greatly extended the geographic focus of campus crime reports. All institutions of higher education receiving federal funds must now provide a geographic breakdown of the crime statistics according to the following categories: (1) on-campus; (2) non-campus building or property; (3) public property immediately adjacent to or running through the university; and (4) dormitories and other residential facilities on campus. Certain non-campus facilities such as fraternity and sorority housing and remote classrooms must also be included in the report. Educational institutions are encouraged to use a map to aid in the disclosure of their crime statistics (Roach, 2000b).

Another question about campus crime data results from whether an arrest is made by the campus police or police from the jurisdiction that contains the campus. The issue here is that local police agencies are not required to even collect, much less report, crime statistics to campus officials for such areas as streets, parking lots and sidewalks running through or adjacent to the campuses. What Congress did not do was give the campus administrators the means to obtain these statistics (Otey, 2000).

The Campus "Community"

Campuses today are beset with behaviors, events and problems that require a sophisticated police presence. In the past, campus "police" were unarmed employees whose primary duty was enforcing curfews and checking security by making sure doors were locked in the evening ("door shakers"). Presently, few campuses have curfews, and door shaking is not considered an important function of campus police. Contemporary campus police administrators have adopted many of the characteristics and techniques of municipal police departments, including armed officers. They also practice problem-solving community-oriented policing techniques and make use of advanced computer technology (Peak, 1995).

Campuses are small, self-contained communities. Although small when compared to the population and geographical size of large cities, a campus of 30,000 or 40,000 students plus faculty and staff may be considered a rather complex entity. Mansour and Sloan (1992) argue that college campuses are communities since they contain the three basic elements of a community: fixed geographic location, common ties among people and social interaction.

However, there are important differences between campuses and what is commonly thought of as a community.

First, consider the age structure of members of this community. Although there are older students, most are recent high school graduates between the ages of 18 and 24. When a cohort of 18-year-old strangers first settles onto a campus, we expect social experimentation as each student searches for his or her niche. Some will engage in excessive alcohol consumption sometimes resulting in violent behavior. Some experiment with illegal drugs. In short, this is the most criminogenic age group in society.

On the other hand, this age group is selected from the least criminogenic high school students in their communities. These are the high-achieving students who have established goals that include higher education. Although they intend to have a good time socially, most are serious about their educational mission and are unlikely to do anything purposefully that would jeopardize this mission.

A second criminogenic aspect of a campus community that separates it from a residential community is its transitory nature. Each fall, new students arrive on campus to mix with the continuing students. Although many students may live on campus during the school year, they often return to their homes during the summer. Furthermore, most do not expect to live on campus beyond the four or five years required to graduate. This makes the student population relatively transitory. Although many take great pride in their universities or colleges, according to the criminology literature transitory populations are not likely to be concerned with long-term improvements in the environment that lead to improved safety (Smith et al., 2000).

A college campus is also criminogenic because its members have predictable routines. Students attend class on a regular basis (hopefully), return to dormitories, and attend sporting and entertainment events. Faculty members also attend (conduct) classes, do research and return to their homes in the evening. Staff members work on campus eight hours a day and return home at night. These routines create a dynamic community of predictable time use, creating many criminal opportunities when books, computers, projectors and personal valuables are left unguarded (Cohen and Felson, 1979; Rengert and Wasilchick, 2000).

Although college campuses are transitory communities with predictable time routines, this does not necessarily translate into a socially disorganized community, comparable to the transition areas of inner cities portrayed by Shaw and McKay (1969). There are many ties among the students, faculty, and staff members based on friendship, social and educational networks. Organizations created and designed to foster interaction among students, such as fraternities and sororities, may strengthen social cohesiveness and lead to lower rates of victimization. For example, Fisher et al. (1998) discovered that membership in a fraternity or sorority reduced the likelihood of experiencing an on-campus theft.

Social cohesiveness does not have to be limited to small groups; it can be campus-wide. One purpose of sporting events is to create a common bond among the campus community members (e.g., we *are* Penn State!). At other times, interaction is less discretionary, as when students meet faculty in class and during office hours, or when public safety staff check IDs before students enter a building. Often social interaction is random, as when students interact in dining halls, libraries and other common spaces. However it may occur, the social interaction evident on campuses mitigates some of the social disorder one might expect from a relatively transitory population.

Further, the members of the campus community are engaged in a common mission — education. This common goal may help develop social and psychological ties among campus members that creates the order within which crime is not likely to flourish (Boyer, 1990). However, if a member of the community does not have education as a goal (for example, a member of an athletic team who intends to turn professional before graduation), he or she may not hesitate to create disorder that makes it more difficult for other community members to attain their goals. Thus, both Bausell et al. (1991) and Fisher et al. (1998) discovered that college athletes were more likely than nonathletes to engage in fights. Some colleges and universities house athletes separately from the remainder of the student body in order to address these and other issues.

One characteristic of a campus that makes it a difficult environment to control is its openness. Campuses typically are park-like settings easily accessible day or night. This openness creates vulnerability since strangers commonly use campus grounds and facilities. The campus community cannot determine who belongs and who does not. In fact, many campus administrators make a point of welcoming everyone. Therefore, a stranger's presence is seldom questioned on campus grounds, creating a less controlled environment.

Nighttime is a particularly vulnerable time on campus. Few people use the campus at this time. Fewer classes are offered, faculty often leave their offices and maintenance schedules are reduced. Predictably, much campus crime takes place late at night when the campus is not heavily used (Siegel and Raymond, 1992).

The use of alcohol and illegal drugs in the evening hours creates an unpredictable environment undermining perceptions of safety on campus. Siegel and Raymond (1992) reported that almost one-third of the undergraduates in their sample reported consuming alcohol at least once a week. Only about 11% of the sample reported complete abstinence from alcohol. Also, over 35% of the sample reported using illegal drugs. Especially vulnerable are women and older members of the community on campus for classes, employment, research, cultural activities and sporting events, who may perceive they are more at risk of becoming a victim of crime due to their smaller physical size (Fisher et al., 1995).

In sum, college and university campuses have many characteristics of a community. Some of these characteristics have been associated with a criminogenic environment (such as age structure and a transitory population). On the other hand, campuses have characteristics not normally found in a residential community that make crime less likely (such as a common educational mission and a specialized public safety or police force). How these forces balance is likely to vary from campus to campus. In fact, there is wide variation in the level of crime between campuses (see Table 1, page 22). Some have attributed the level of safety to the type of student attending the school (Fernandez and Lizotte, 1995), while others have likened campus safety to the criminogenic nature of the community surrounding the campus (APBnews.com, 1999; McPheters, 1978). The question of whether the campus community is part of a larger community that contributes to the level of crime on campus has been the focus of recent debate. In the next chapter, we examine this issue in detail.

Chapter II.
The Campus Community Within Its Setting

APBnews.com, a web-based news provider, released a special report titled "College Community Crime" in 1999 that allowed users to determine the risk of violent crime for 1,497 college communities (Letham, 2000). This first nationwide crime risk survey of all four-year college and university communities in the United States included an analysis of the neighborhoods that surround a campus community. The neighborhoods, as defined in this study, consisted of all areas within one mile of each campus. The authors of this study assumed that campus residents use this surrounding area and therefore were at risk of victimization, and/or that criminals from this surrounding area traveled onto campus to locate victims. The analysis did not claim to test the degree to which either assumption is valid.

CAP Index, Inc., the nation's leading provider of crime risk data to corporate America, conducted the analysis for APBnews.com. CAP Index, Inc. computed campus community crime risk factors by correlating socioeconomic neighborhood data with (a) reported crime data obtained from the Uniform Crime Reports published by the Federal Bureau of Investigation, and (b) victimization surveys collected by the Bureau of Justice Statistics. These data were supplemented by crime incident reports from various police departments and corporate clients. The socioeconomic data include 21 variables, such as real estate values and population density (Letham, 2000). The data were aggregated to the census tract level.

These data raise the issue of whether the community setting within which the campus is located determines the risk of victimization on campus. In other words, can we use risk factors for a larger area to determine the risk of a smaller community within this larger community? Pearson and Toby (1991:117) seem to imply that we can. They state that college campuses are characterized by the following risk factors: (1) *targets* — students, faculty, and staff who create a large pool of potential targets; (2) *physical location* — many university campuses are bordered by transitional neighborhoods with low socioeconomic characteristics, a place where one could expect to find disproportionate numbers of prospective offenders in residence; and (3) *lack of security* — low levels of security are generally associated with college campuses. These authors feel that campuses characterized by all three risk factors pose the greatest opportunities for victimization.

Characteristics of Targets

All three of the above factors are open to debate since Pearson and Toby (1991) do not provide evidence beyond armchair reasoning to substantiate their assertions. For example, do students, faculty, and staff members exemplify characteristics that would make them more vulnerable to crime than any other member of the larger community? Is there something about them that would attract a criminal's attention more so than a resident within the surrounding community? The answers are not clear. Common sense would lead us to believe that students are easy prey because they often act as poor guardians of themselves and their property (Fernandez and Lizotte, 1995). They commonly leave book bags unattended in study rooms and walk alone along corridors and alleys. Furthermore, students' consumption of alcohol might interfere with their ability to assess a dangerous situation or to defend themselves. Potential offenders may consider campuses and students low-risk targets compared to other targets within their residential community, where discovery and punishment are more likely. If students' naivete and campus lifestyle (18 to 24 year olds searching for a niche in society) make them targets, it would be reasonable to assume that crime would spill over from the community onto the campus (Hakim and Rengert, 1981). But is this the case?

When we move from armchair theorizing to actual case studies, we are forced to reevaluate some of our assumptions. For example, Bromley (1992), Fox and Hellman (1985), and Lizotte and Fernandez (1993) discovered that the rate of crime on campus was generally much lower than that of its surrounding community. Perhaps students are not targeted to the extent that Pearson and Toby (1991) would have us believe.

Moreover, there is evidence that the type of student is related to the level of victimization. Again, we are forced to reexamine some of our common-sense assumptions or perhaps prejudices. For example, Fernandez and Lizotte (1995) discovered that campuses dominated by commuter students (often located within cities) had lower rates of campus student victimization than residential campuses (often located in leafy suburbs or rural areas). This makes sense since the number of hours at risk of victimization on campus are far fewer for a commuter student than for a residential student. Also, commuter students are less likely to be on campus during the late night hours — a time associated with more criminal activity (Siegel and Raymond, 1992). Furthermore, the commuter student usually does not bring onto campus expensive electronic recreational equipment such as radios, televisions, and compact disk players.

The second surprising finding concerns the more costly schools. Fernandez and Lizotte (1995) discovered that one of the strongest and most consistent correlates of campus crime rates was a measure of wealth of the students. Campuses with higher room and board costs had higher rates of all forms of crime associated with an economic motive. Fisher et al. (1998) may have explained this phenomenon by measuring student wealth more directly. In a victimization survey, those students who spent larger sums of money per week on nonessentials (e.g., entertainment, recreation, restaurants) had a higher risk of on-campus theft victimization than those who did not.

Fox and Hellman (1985) measured the financial characteristics of a campus by faculty salaries, the cost of tuition and room and board, and the percentage of students receiving financial aid. They discovered that the financial characteristics of a campus were positively and significantly related to crime. These authors also measured educational quality by the percentage of graduate students, the competitiveness of the school from Barron's guide, and the percentage of the faculty with the Ph.D. or other terminal degree. Here again, the finding was counterintuitive; a higher quality of education was associated with higher crime rates. The association was attributed to economic reasons as well: "a high-quality education generally costs more, so that quality is positively correlated with the economic status of the students and the value of campus assets...." (Fox and Hellman, 1985:438). Both sets of authors reasoned that wealthier students might have more expensive possessions to steal at comparatively little risk to the offender. In any case, campuses with more affordable costs and those with a lower quality education, which presumably attract students from lower socioeconomic backgrounds, in fact have lower property crime rates than their counterparts.

Physical Location of the Campus

The second factor considered by Pearson and Toby (1991) is the physical location of university campuses. Many schools are located in transitional neighborhoods with low socioeconomic characteristics. Often, a disproportionate number of prospective offenders live in these neighborhoods. APBnews.com (1999) equated the level of criminal activity in the surrounding community with the level of safety of the college student. Again, this seems to make sense intuitively. If many potential criminals live in the surrounding area, the probability of a student's becoming a victim of crime should increase (Felson, 1986). In fact, this agrees with a central premise of the "routine activities" theory of victimization (Cohen and Felson, 1979).

Important issues surround this expectation. First, how far out should one go from campus and still expect the "potential criminal" to focus his attention on the campus as a search area for crime sites? In the APBnews.com (1999) study, the analyst used a radius of one mile. This assumes either that the potential criminal is willing to travel a mile for crime, or that students routinely use the residential communities up to a mile from campus. In the first instance, the distance to crime is going to depend on the mode of transportation used by the criminal. When on foot, Rengert (1996) discovered that the vast majority of crimes occurred within three blocks of the criminal's anchor point (home, drug sales area, school, etc.). Turner (1969) discovered that the mean distance traveled by juveniles in Philadelphia to crime was 0.4 miles. When an automobile is used, as is common in suburban and rural areas, the distances will be further. However, in low socioeconomic transition areas of cities, those committing the vast majority of crime (juveniles) are not likely to have access to an automobile. Therefore, it is not likely that they will walk one mile (about 10 or 11 city blocks) to commit a crime when opportunities exist closer to home.

The same reasoning holds true for college students. Those who do not live on campus and are not commuting students will want to live as close to campus as possible — two to three blocks, not 10 to 11 blocks. Furthermore, their social activities will be oriented toward campus and not the other direction. They are not likely to wander 10 or 11 blocks on foot in the opposite direction from campus in an urban setting.

A second problem stems from the well-documented "ecological fallacy." In simple terms, the ecological fallacy means that one cannot average the crime risks over a larger community and assume that a smaller community contained within it experiences this average crime risk. In fact, one characteristic of a mean (or an average) is that it may not exist in *any* of the areas its figures are derived from. For example, let's assume that four areas have been scaled to have crime risks of 2, 4, 4 and 10. When we average these figures, we get a crime risk of 5, which does not exist in any of these sub-areas. A second characteristic of a mean is that it is unduly affected by extreme values: 5 is higher than three of the areas and lower than just one in the above example. Therefore, one cannot take the crime risk of the entire area and assume it exists in any small part of the area. However, this is exactly what APBnews.com (1999) did when it ranked the campuses by their crime risks computed from the surrounding communities.

Fernandez and Lizotte (1995) completed the most comprehensive study of the relationship of the characteristics of the surrounding community to campus crime. They not only tested the impact of the surrounding community on campus crime, but also the impact of campus characteristics on crime in the surrounding community (e.g., drunken students perhaps). For each type of crime, the authors used three-stage least squares simultaneous equations to estimate the reciprocal relationships between campus and community crime, controlling for the characteristics of both the campus and the community. The hypothesis of the model is that the demographic and economic characteristics of both campus and the surrounding community would affect campus crime rates *and* community crime rates in a causal loop. The results are surprising and clear. In general, community crime rates *and* community characteristics had little effect on campus crime rates. Campus characteristics, on the other hand, had strong and consistent effects on campus crime rates. Therefore, it's not the community surrounding the campus; it's the campus proper that is important for safety. The only exceptions found were robbery and motor vehicle theft, whose rates in the surrounding community did affect the robbery and motor vehicle theft rate on campus. The authors reason that these were likely to have been committed by criminals from the surrounding community who targeted both students and community residents. These were also the two crimes that criminals were likely to travel the farthest to commit (Capone and Nichols, 1976; McIver, 1981). Other crimes on campus were more likely to be committed by students targeting other students. Sloan (1994) notes that over 80% of reported campus crimes involved students victimizing other students and over 95% of all offenses committed on college and university campuses involved alcohol or drugs.

Doubters will question whether one study is enough to draw the conclusion that the crime rate or the socioeconomic characteristics of the surrounding community generally have little influence on the risk of victimization on campus. However, Fox and Hellman (1985) examined the relative risk of crime on campus vis-à-vis their communities to determine whether the risk varied by location within and outside metropolitan areas. This was the first study to specifically focus on the safety of urban campuses, many of which are surrounded by relatively low socioeconomic neighborhoods as compared to their non-metropolitan counterparts. The authors analyzed 222 colleges and universities. Thirty-five percent of the campuses were located outside of a Standard Metropolitan Statistical Area (SMSA), 29% were located in a suburban area or a minor city in an SMSA, and 36% were located within a major city in an SMSA. Rates of crime were calculated by taking the ratio of offenses to full-time equivalent student enrollment plus faculty and scaled by one thousand.

Over all, the ratio of campus index crimes per 1,000 students and faculty to crimes in the community within which the campus is located per 1,000 residents was much less than one (0.58). Thus, campuses were much safer than the communities that contained them.

Next, Fox and Hellman (1985) examined the outliers, those campuses that were much safer than their surrounding communities as well as those that were much more dangerous. The crime rate of the safest campus with respect to the surrounding community was only 1% of the surrounding community's crime rate. The campus that was the most dangerous compared to the surrounding community had a crime rate almost three times that of the community. Twenty campuses had crime rates that exceeded the crime rate in the community in which they were located. However, these relatively dangerous campuses were not located in major cities where they attracted a plethora of criminals as one might expect. Rather, they were in non-metropolitan areas with low crime rates in the surrounding neighborhoods. In fact, urban campuses were much safer than their non-SMSA counterparts when compared to the surrounding community. However, this statement leaves unresolved the question of whether the ratio is high in non-SMSA campus-community locations because the denominator of the ratio (community) is lower than normal or the numerator (campus) is higher than normal. When Fox and Hellman (1985) examined this issue they discovered that the location of a campus appeared to have no association with the campus crime rate. The crime rate in the surrounding community had little or no impact on campus crime rates.

Fox and Hellman (1985:433) concluded:

> This surprising result — that urban, suburban, and rural campuses have similar rates of crime, on the average — suggests either that there is no influence of the community on campus crime or that the influence of the community is uniform per capita across locational types…Thus the locational pattern observed in the ratio of campus to community crime is due simply to a locational pattern in community crime rates.

Fisher et al. (1998) noted that one cannot assume that potential criminals living anywhere in the community containing a campus will know about or feel comfortable committing a crime on campus. They restricted their analysis to census tracts contiguous to a campus boundary. In a multilevel analysis, they found that census tract variables did not predict on-campus victimization. They point out that this finding might well indicate that college campuses are, to a degree, "ivory towers."

This is a surprising finding that many have trouble accepting, as exemplified by the APBnews.com (1999)-commissioned survey, which ignored the campus side of the equation by concentrating entirely on the characteristics of the surrounding community. On the other hand, the APBnews.com analysis focused only on the rarest of crimes that occur on campus — violent offenses. Yet, in his analysis of 543 campuses, Sloan (1985) noted that serious violence accounted for less than 2% of the total crime reported on the campuses. As the community becomes more urban, the mix of crime becomes more violent (Fox and Hellman, 1985), but the increased proportion of violent crime does not affect the total crime rate because serious violent crime is rare on American campuses when compared to total crime.

Sloan (1994) examined the mix of crime on campus as it relates to the surrounding neighborhoods. His analysis sheds light on whether violent and property crime are related to characteristics of the surrounding community. Sloan (1994) divided 543 campuses into four categories based on the communities in which they were located: (1) rural areas; (2) small towns; (3) city setting; and (4) metropolitan setting. In a factor analysis of 19 variables, none were related to the campus variable. Next, Sloan (1994) constructed four campus crime ratios: (1) theft and burglary rate; (2) violence rate; (3) drinking/drug rate; and (4) vandalism rate per 1,000 students and faculty. When the community setting of the campuses was examined with respect to these four crime rates, only violence was positively related at the .05 level of significance. Interestingly, drinking and drug use arrests were negatively related to campus setting. The other crime rates and the total crime rate were not significantly related to the campus setting.

Finally, Bromley (1999) focused entirely on community colleges to determine the rates of property and violent crimes on particular community college campuses, in comparison to rates in the cities that surround them. Data were obtained for 31 community colleges and their host cities, and crime rates per 1,000 population were computed for each. When the community college overall index crime rates were compared with that of their host cities, all but one community college had substantially lower rates. The exception was Contra Costa Community College in San Pablo, California, which had an exceptionally high campus crime rate. Contra Costa Community College's crime rate was over four times higher than the crime rate of the next highest community college (Holyoke Community College in Holyoke, MA). Thus, Contra Costa Community College was clearly an outlier. In all sets of comparisons, the community colleges had lower violent crime rates than the communities that contained them. The proportion of violent crimes in the community was four times higher than the proportion of violent crimes on community college campuses. These findings support those of Bromley (1992), who studied four-year campuses and discovered that violent crimes comprised 2% of all offenses committed on campus as compared to 18% of all offenses committed in the communities containing the campuses. Other researchers have found the same crime mix ratio on campuses and their community settings (Bromley, 1995; Stormer and Senorath, 1992).

Clearly, campuses are not the havens of violence the media would sometimes have us believe (Surette, 1992). This is clearly contrary to what Smith and Smith (1990) and APBnews.com (1999) suggest.

Campus and College Community Crime Rates

We conclude this section with our own analysis of the relationship of campus crime rates with that of the surrounding neighborhoods. In this case, we can directly assess the APBnews.com (1999) assumption that the characteristics of the neighborhoods surrounding a campus affect the level of safety for college students. We focus entirely on violent crime rates. Two sources of data are available to us. The first is the ranking of colleges by their level of safety conducted by APBnews.com, which examined only the characteristics of neighborhoods surrounding the campus. In comparison, data on crime that occurs on campus have been reported by the campus administrators and published in the *Chronicle of Higher Education* (1999).

Both sources of data are subject to the criticism that they rely on "reported" crime statistics. APBnews.com relied partly on data reported by police departments to the Federal Bureau of Investigation and published in the Uniform Crime Reports. The *Chronicle of Higher Education* data are based on reports from campus administrators as required in The Student Right-to-Know laws of many states and the federal government. Both sets of data are subject to bias. However, both have been scrutinized for accuracy.

Both the Uniform Crime Reports and data reported by campus administrators have problems identifying and justifying the boundary of their enumeration areas. In the case of the Uniform Crime Reports, the data for central cities reflect political boundaries that in the case of old East Coast cities have not changed in over 100 years. As the metropolitan area continues to grow outward, this politically-bounded city contains less and less of the metropolitan area. The census bureau has attempted to correct this by constructing Standard Metropolitan Statistical Areas (SMSA), which include the central city plus contiguously built up suburban counties. In this case, metropolitan areas can contain rural areas on the outskirts of the suburban county. Nevertheless, there is no completely satisfactory means of delineating a city or a metropolitan area.

Similarly, there is no completely satisfactory means of delineating a campus community. Many campuses have entry gates (see Figure 1), fences or walls to demarcate their campuses. However, many colleges and universities own and/or use facilities scattered throughout the surrounding community beyond these campus boundaries. There is a question of whether or not these outlying facilities should be considered part of the campus, especially when reporting campus crime. The Student Right-to-Know Act is clear that they must be included.

Figure 1: Entry Gate to a College Campus

The problem is even more complex in the case of mixed-use facilities. What if there is a private commercial establishment on the first floor of a building and campus offices on the second and higher floors. Should a crime that occurs in the commercial establishment be counted as a campus crime? Does it make a difference if the university owns the entire building and the lower floor is leased to the commercial establishment? This is exactly the debate faced by the University of Pennsylvania. The administrators of the University of Pennsylvania excluded from its tallies crimes that occurred in portions of university buildings used for commercial purposes, usually ground-floor storefronts. The controversy centered on a Penn-owned building at the corner of 34th and Walnut Streets that either is on or adjoins the campus, depending on the definition of the campus boundary. Known as the "3401 Building," the six-story structure housed the university's departments of history, American civilization and cognitive sciences on the upper floors. The ground level was leased to retail businesses known collectively as "The Shops at Penn." If a crime occurred on one of these ground floor establishments, Penn did not count it as a "campus crime." If a crime occurred on any floor above the ground level, Penn designated it a campus crime. The University of Pennsylvania's method of defining its campus was reviewed and found acceptable by the United States Department of Education (Matza, 1998).

Not everyone agreed with the University of Pennsylvania's and the United States Department of Education's definition of a campus. Figure 2 illustrates crimes that were counted as off-campus and those that were counted as campus crimes. To the casual observer, the fact that spatial clusters of crime contain both on-campus and off-campus crimes does not make sense. Furthermore, the crimes occurring in and around the Food Court and Shops at Penn at 34th and Walnut Streets (just below and to the left of the Key in Figure 2) seem to be on the university's campus. Senator Arlen Specter (R, PA.), a 1951 Penn graduate takes exception to how the University counted these crimes: "I know 34th and Walnut....Its not only on campus, it's also ... owned by the University" (quoted by Matza, 1998, p.1). Therefore, if we use the 1990 official definition of a campus, crimes in the same spatial location could be both on-campus crimes in facilities on upper floors of a building and off-campus crimes in facilities on the ground floor or sidewalk. The 1998 Amendment to the 1990 Campus Security Act clarifies these issues. The University of Pennsylvania will now be required to count crimes occurring in the Food Court and Shops at Penn as campus crimes.

Not all campuses have crime statistics reported in the *Chronicle of Higher Education*. For example, the *Chronicle* does not collect statistics from institutions with fewer than 5,000 students. Therefore, we analyzed data for only

Figure 2: Campus and Non-campus Street Robberies
at the University of Pennsylvania

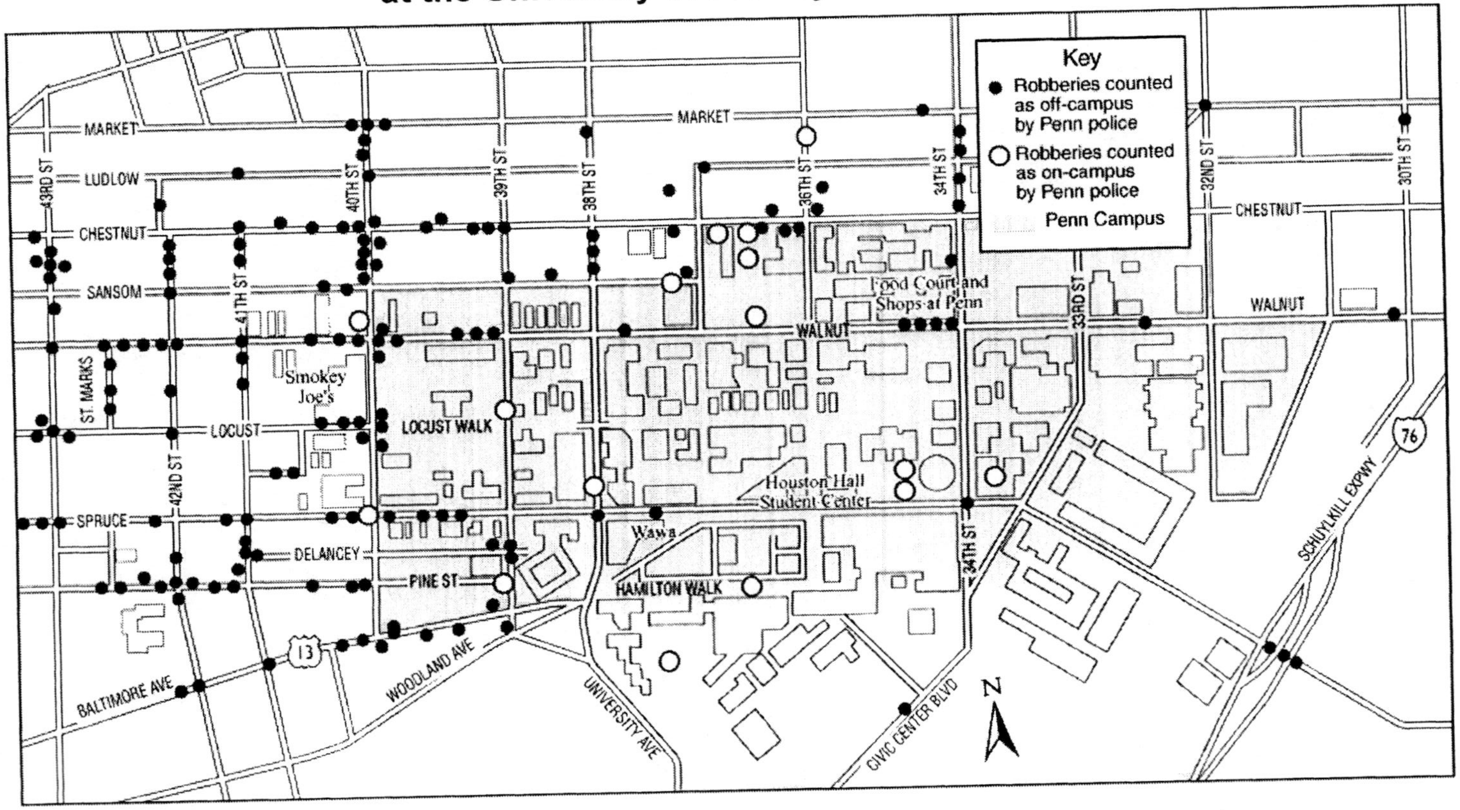

those 470 colleges that occurred in both sources of data. APBnews.com (1999) ranked the colleges in their report by level of safety in the surrounding neighborhoods. We computed the rate of violent crime per 1,000 students and faculty on each campus and then ranked the 470 colleges from the *Chronicle of Higher Education* that also occurred in the APBnews.com series. In Table 1, we list the campuses in the order of their rank by APBnews.com from the safest to the least safe campus and note the difference in this rank to that of the *Chronicle of Higher Education*.

We conducted a Spearman's rank-order correlation between the two series of data. The result was a rank order coefficient of -.52 that was not statistically significant at the .05 level or higher. When we compared differences in ranks, we found four campuses that ranked 400 points lower on the *Chronicle* than on the APBnews.com rank. This implies that these campuses were much more dangerous than their surrounding communities. Note that none of these campuses was located in large metropolitan areas. The surrounding neighborhoods were considered relatively safe although their campuses did not reflect these neighborhood characteristics. The other side of the coin were the six campuses in which the *Chronicle* ranks were more than 400 points lower than the APBnews.com (1999) ranks. These campuses were safer than their surrounding communities. Note that the majority of these campuses were in large metropolitan areas such as New York City, Chicago and San Francisco.

The fact that the two series were negatively correlated and not significantly related implies that characteristics of neighborhoods surrounding college campuses did not translate directly into campus safety in terms of violent crime on campus. Perhaps, then, we should rethink Pearson and Toby's (1991) second proposition that the physical setting of a campus strongly influences the level of student safety on campus.

Table 1: Campuses Ranked from Safest to Least Safe

School Name	City	State	APB	Chronicle	Difference
Richard Stockton College of New Jersey	Pomona	NJ	1	251	-250.00
Quinnipiac College	Hamden	CT	2	1	1.00
University of Southern Maine	Gorham	ME	3	130	-127.00
University of Wisconsin, River Falls	River Falls	WI	4	240	-236.00
Dowling College	Oakdale	NY	5	1	4.00
University of Southern Indiana	Evansville	IN	6	168	-162.00
State University of NY College at Cortland	Cortland	NY	6	124	-118.00
Bowie State University	Bowie	MD	8	437	-429.00
State University of NY College at Oswego	Oswego	NY	9	425	-416.00
University of Tennessee at Martin	Martin	TN	10	464	-454.00
Lincoln Christian College and Seminary	Lincoln	IL	11	294	-283.00
State University of NY College at Oneonta	Oneonta	NY	12	295	-283.00
Liberty University	Lynchburg	VA	12	32	-20.00
University of Maine at Augusta	Augusta	ME	12	1	11.00
University of Maine	Orono	ME	15	356	-341.00
Slippery Rock University	Slippery Rock	PA	15	215	-200.00
State University of NY at Stony Brook	Stony Brook	NY	17	297	-280.00
Rider University	Lawrenceville	NJ	17	245	-228.00
New Hampshire College	Manchester	NH	19	1	18.00
Indiana University Southeast	New Albany	IN	19	1	18.00
Frostburg State University	Frostburg	MD	21	410	-389.00
East Stroudsburg University	E. Stroudsburg	PA	22	430	-408.00
Mercy College	Dobbs Ferry	NY	22	36	-14.00
University of Nebraska at Kearney	Kearney	NE	24	103	-79.00
Ashland University	Ashland	OH	24	1	23.00
Park College	Parkville	MO	26	32	-6.00
University of Wisconsin, Oshkosh	Oshkosh	WI	27	373	-346.00
University of Wisconsin, Stevens Point	Stevens Point	WI	27	184	-157.00
Bridgewater State College	Bridgewater	MA	29	399	-370.00
University of Delaware	Newark	DE	30	353	-323.00
University of Massachusetts, Dartmouth	N. Dartmouth	MA	31	387	-356.00
Rowan University	Glassboro	NJ	31	337	-306.00

School Name	City	State	APB	Chronicle	Difference
Saginaw Valley State	University Ctr	MI	31	262	-231.00
Southern Illinois University	Edwardsville	IL	31	211	-180.00
George Mason University	Fairfax	VA	31	174	-143.00
California State University, Bakersfield	Bakersfield	CA	36	350	-314.00
University of South Dakota	Vermillion	SD	37	283	-246.00
Winona State University	Winona	MN	37	114	-77.00
State University of NY College at Geneseo	Geneseo	NY	39	260	-221.00
Pepperdine University	Malibu	CA	39	178	-139.00
Fairmont State College	Fairmont	WV	39	1	38.00
Missouri Western State College	St. Joseph	MO	42	428	-386.00
Saint Mary's University of Minnesota	Winona	MN	42	89	-47.00
University of Vermont	Burlington	VT	42	80	-38.00
California University of Pennsylvania	California	PA	45	191	-146.00
Bloomsburg University of Pennsylvania	Bloomsburg	PA	45	107	-62.00
University of Wisconsin, Green Bay	Green Bay	WI	47	52	-5.00
University of North Dakota	Grand Forks	ND	48	308	-260.00
Fairleigh Dickinson University, Madison	Madison	NJ	49	407	-358.00
Pittsburg State University	Pittsburg	KS	49	84	-35.00
Saint Cloud State University	St. Cloud	MN	51	396	-345.00
Princeton University	Princeton	NJ	51	365	-314.00
Eastern Illinois University	Charleston	IL	51	218	-167.00
University of Missouri Rolla	Rolla	MO	54	337	-283.00
University of Wisconsin, Platteville	Platteville	WI	54	200	-146.00
Shippensburg University of Pennsylvania	Shippensburg	PA	56	259	-203.00
Oklahoma State University	Stillwater	OK	56	162	-106.00
Murray State University	Murray	KY	58	434	-376.00
University of Rhode Island	Kingston	RI	58	229	-171.00
West Texas A&M University	Canyon	TX	58	42	16.00
Illinois State University	Normal	IL	61	426	-365.00
Northern Illinois University	DeKalb	IL	61	375	-314.00
Bentley College	Waltham	MA	61	361	-300.00
Dartmouth College	Hanover	NH	61	341	-280.00
University of Connecticut	Storrs	CT	61	277	-216.00
Mankato State University	Mankato	MN	61	220	-159.00
Marshall University	Huntington	WV	61	198	-137.00

School Name	City	State	APB	Chronicle	Difference
Eastern Washington University	Cheney	WA	68	235	-167.00
Armstrong Atlantic State University	Savannah	GA	68	139	-71.00
Idaho State University	Pocatello	ID	68	67	1.00
College of William and Mary	Williamsburg	VA	68	455	-387.00
University of Colorado, Colorado Springs	Col. Springs	CO	68	416	-348.00
State University of NY, Brockport	Brockport	NY	68	276	-208.00
James Madison University	Harrisonburg	VA	74	422	-348.00
Montana State University, Bozeman	Bozeman	MT	74	328	-254.00
Edinboro University of Pennsylvania	Edinboro	PA	74	73	1.00
Central Missouri State University	Warrensburg	MO	74	73	1.00
Missouri Southern State College	Joplin	MO	78	244	-166.00
Kutztown University	Kutztown	PA	79	444	-365.00
University of Wisconsin, Whitewater	Whitewater	WI	79	121	-42.00
University of Oklahoma	Norman	OK	81	311	-230.00
University of Central Oklahoma	Edmond	OK	81	196	-115.00
Western Carolina University	Cullowhee	NC	83	427	-344.00
Appalachian State University	Boone	NC	83	315	-232.00
West Virginia University	Morgantown	WV	85	157	-72.00
University of Central Arkansas	Conway	AR	85	146	-61.00
Texas A&M University at Commerce	Commerce	TX	85	106	-21.00
Sacred Heart University	Fairfield	CT	85	56	29.00
East Tennessee State University	Johnson City	TN	89	182	-93.00
State University of NY, New Paltz	New Paltz	NY	89	179	-90.00
Indiana University of Pennsylvania	Indiana	PA	91	371	-280.00
University of Maine at Farmington	Farmington	ME	91	356	-265.00
Eastern Kentucky University	Richmond	KY	91	194	-103.00
Truman State University	Kirksville	MO	91	82	9.00
University of Southern Colorado	Pueblo	CO	91	62	29.00
Radford University	Radford	VA	96	435	-339.00
University of New Hampshire	Durham	NH	96	279	-183.00
Sonoma State University	Rohnert Park	CA	96	219	-123.00
Saint Leo College	Saint Leo	FL	96	1	95.00
Midwestern State University	Witicha Falls	TX	100	360	-260.00
Miami University	Oxford	OH	100	239	-139.00
University of Wyoming	Laramie	WY	100	207	-107.00

School Name	City	State	APB	Chronicle	Difference
University of Wisconsin, Stout	Menomonie	WI	100	142	-42.00
Clarion University of Pennsylvania	Clarion	PA	104	390	-286.00
Central Michigan University	Mt. Pleasant	MI	105	243	-138.00
Kennesaw State University	Kennesaw	GA	105	86	19.00
University of North Carolina, Chapel Hill	Chapel Hill	NC	107	462	-355.00
Northwest Missouri State University	Maryville	MO	107	431	-324.00
University of Texas at San Antonio	San Antonio	TX	107	134	-27.00
State University of NY, Binghamton	Binghamton	NY	110	310	-200.00
Grand Valley State University	Allendale	MI	111	108	3.00
Kent State University	Kent	OH	111	61	50.00
University of Central Florida	Orlando	FL	113	79	34.00
Florida Christian College	Kissimmee	FL	114	386	-272.00
Michigan Technological University	Houghton	MI	114	125	-11.00
Cameron University	Lawton	OK	114	1	113.00
Fitchburg State College	Fitchburg	MA	117	204	-87.00
North Dakota State	Fargo	ND	118	378	-260.00
Moorhead State University	Moorhead	MN	118	324	-206.00
Ball State University	Muncie	IN	118	257	-139.00
University of North Florida	Jacksonville	FL	118	72	46.00
Clemson University	Clemson	SC	122	368	-246.00
Western Illinois University	Macomb	IL	122	228	-106.00
Indiana Univ.-Purdue Univ., Fort Wayne	Fort Wayne	IN	122	98	24.00
Southeast Missouri State University	Cp. Girardeau	MO	122	96	26.00
University of Iowa	Iowa City	IA	126	211	-85.00
Western Washington University	Bellingham	WA	126	71	55.00
Ferris State University	Big Rapids	MI	128	454	-326.00
Campbell University	Buies Creek	NC	129	317	-188.00
Cardinal Stritch University	Milwaukee	WI	129	93	36.00
Ohio University	Athens	OH	131	247	-116.00
University of California, San Diego	La Jolla	CA	132	192	-60.00
Auburn University, Montgomery	Montgomery	AL	132	138	-6.00
University of Massachusetts, Amherst	Amherst	MA	134	411	-277.00
South Dakota State University	Brookings	SD	134	222	-88.00
Indiana University at South Bend	South Bend	IN	136	190	-54.00
McNeese State University	Lake Charles	LA	137	359	-222.00

School Name	City	State	APB	Chronicle	Difference
National University	La Jolla	CA	138	26	112.00
Indiana State University	Terre Haute	IN	139	393	-254.00
Long Island University, C.W. Post Campus	Brookville	NY	140	320	-180.00
University of Texas at Dallas	Richardson	TX	140	166	-26.00
Boise State University	Boise	ID	140	1	139.00
Utah State University	Logan	UT	143	161	-18.00
Austin Peay State University	Clarkesville	TN	144	127	17.00
University of Kansas	Lawrence	KS	145	313	-168.00
University of Northern Iowa	Cedar Falls	IA	145	286	-141.00
University of Utah	Salt Lake City	UT	147	307	-160.00
Washburn University of Topeka	Topeka	KS	147	270	-123.00
Iowa State University	Ames	IA	147	167	-20.00
Brigham Young University	Provo	UT	147	142	5.00
State University of NY, Plattsburgh	Plattsburgh	NY	151	252	-101.00
Colorado State University	Fort Collins	CO	152	429	-277.00
Tufts University	Medford	MA	152	340	-188.00
Indiana University at Bloomington	Bloomington	IN	152	292	-140.00
Tarleton State University	Stephenville	TX	152	44	108.00
Lesley College	Cambridge	MA	152	1	151.00
Penn State Univ., University Park Campus	University Park	PA	157	181	-24.00
Bowling Green State University	Bowling Green	OH	157	110	47.00
University of Missouri, Columbia	Columbia	MO	159	284	-125.00
Southwest Missouri State University	Springfield	MO	159	205	-46.00
Villanova University	Villanova	PA	161	330	-169.00
Montana State University, Billings	Billings	MT	161	328	-167.00
Adams State College	Alamosa	CO	163	296	-133.00
State University of NY, Buffalo	Buffalo	NY	164	395	-231.00
University of Oregon	Eugene	OR	164	253	-89.00
University of West Florida	Pensacola	FL	166	132	34.00
Wright State University	Dayton	OH	166	121	45.00
University of Notre Dame	Notre Dame	IN	168	153	15.00
College of New Rochelle, School of New Resources	New Rochelle	NY	168	1	167.00
College of New Rochelle	New Rochelle	NY	168	1	167.00
Southern Utah University	Cedar City	UT	171	466	-295.00
University of Arkansas at Fayetteville	Fayetteville	AR	171	265	-94.00

School Name	City	State	APB	Chronicle	Difference
Virginia Polytechnic Institute and State University	Blacksburg	VA	173	418	-245.00
Jacksonville State University	Jacksonville	AL	173	103	70.00
Emporia State University	Emporia	KS	173	50	123.00
Kansas State University	Manhattan	KS	176	199	-23.00
University of Minnesota, Duluth	Duluth	MN	176	63	113.00
Iona College	New Rochelle	NY	176	59	117.00
California State University, Stanislaus	Turlock	CA	179	214	-35.00
University of Wisconsin, Eau Claire	Eau Claire	WI	179	197	-18.00
Tennessee Technological University	Cookeville	TN	181	376	-195.00
University of Idaho	Moscow	ID	181	140	41.00
University of Virginia	Charlottesville	VA	183	316	-133.00
Rensselaer Polytechnic Institute	Troy	NY	184	298	-114.00
Western Kentucky University	Bowling Green	KY	184	108	76.00
Cornell University	Ithaca	NY	186	370	-184.00
NY Institute of Technology, Old Westbury	Old Westbury	NY	186	220	-34.00
Michigan State University	East Lansing	MI	188	424	-236.00
Columbia College	Columbia	MO	189	1	188.00
Southern Illinois University at Carbondale	Carbondale	IL	190	445	-255.00
University of Michigan, Ann Arbor	Ann Arbor	MI	190	385	-195.00
Troy State University, Dothan	Dothan	AL	190	168	22.00
University of Northern Colorado	Greeley	CO	193	261	-68.00
Washington State University	Pullman	WA	193	156	37.00
University of California, Irvine	Irvine	CA	195	362	-167.00
Northeastern State University	Tahlequah	OK	196	352	-156.00
Sam Houston State University	Huntsville	TX	197	45	152.00
Angelo State University	San Angelo	TX	197	45	152.00
Central Washington University	Ellensburg	WA	199	300	-101.00
University of Mississippi	University	MS	200	95	105.00
University of Wisconsin, La Crosse	LaCrosse	WI	201	177	24.00
Providence College	Providence	RI	202	52	150.00
City University of NY, Queens College	Flushing	NY	203	24	179.00
Hampton University	Hampton	VA	204	460	-256.00
Oregon State University	Corvallis	OR	205	440	-235.00
West Chester University	West Chester	PA	206	309	-103.00

School Name	City	State	APB	Chronicle	Difference
University of California, Davis	Davis	CA	207	321	-114.00
University of Alaska, Fairbanks	Fairbanks	AK	208	414	-206.00
Salisbury State University	Salisbury	MD	209	388	-179.00
Georgia College and State University	Milledgeville	GA	209	54	155.00
University of Nebraska, Lincoln	Lincoln	NE	211	423	-212.00
University of Nebraska, Omaha	Omaha	NE	211	37	174.00
Webster University	St. Louis	MO	213	69	144.00
Worcester State College	Worcester	MA	214	57	157.00
Humboldt State University	Arcata	CA	215	302	-87.00
University of Montana	Missoula	MT	216	155	61.00
University of Illinois, Urbana-Champaign	Urbana	IL	217	384	-167.00
Ithaca College	Ithaca	NY	218	258	-40.00
Middle Tennessee State	Murfreesboro	TN	219	453	-234.00
University of Alaska, Anchorage	Anchorage	AK	220	30	190.00
Fairleigh Dickinson Teaneck, Hackensack	Teaneck	NJ	221	407	-186.00
Arkansas State University	State Univ.	AR	221	270	-49.00
University of Texas at Arlington	Arlington	TX	223	201	22.00
California State University, Hayward	Hayward	CA	224	188	36.00
Adelphi University	Garden City	NY	224	49	175.00
Salem State College	Salem	MA	226	441	-215.00
Lehigh University	Bethlehem	PA	227	439	-212.00
Northern Kentucky University	Highland Hghts.	KY	228	137	91.00
Loyola Marymount University	Los Angeles	CA	229	333	-104.00
Harvard University, Harvard and Radcliffe Colleges	Cambridge	MA	230	382	-152.00
University of Tennessee at Knoxville	Knoxville	TN	231	343	-112.00
California State University, Chico	Chico	CA	231	148	83.00
Nicholls State University	Thibodaux	LA	233	37	196.00
City University of NY, College of Staten Island	Staten Island	NY	234	90	144.00
Troy State University	Troy	AL	235	168	67.00
California State Polytech University, Pomona	Pomona	CA	236	272	-36.00
University of California, Santa Barbara	Santa Barbara	CA	237	189	48.00
University of Colorado at Boulder	Boulder	CO	238	303	-65.00
Morgan State University	Baltimore	MD	239	470	-231.00

School Name	City	State	APB	Chronicle	Difference
Mississippi State University	Mississippi State	MS	239	242	-3.00
Western Connecticut State University	Danbury	CT	239	97	142.00
Morehead State University	Morehead	KY	242	364	-122.00
York College of Pennsylvania	York	PA	243	205	38.00
University of California, Santa Cruz	Santa Cruz	CA	244	327	-83.00
Prairie View A&M University	Prairie View	TX	245	457	-212.00
Youngstown State University	Youngstown	OH	246	103	143.00
Montclair State University	Upper Montclair	NJ	247	232	15.00
University of North Alabama	Florence	AL	247	142	105.00
University of San Diego	San Diego	CA	249	286	-37.00
Louisiana Tech University	Ruston	LA	249	141	108.00
Texas Tech University	Lubbock	TX	251	76	175.00
State University of West Georgia	Carrollton	GA	252	240	12.00
Millersville University of Pennsylvania	Millersville	PA	253	367	-114.00
New Mexico State University	Las Cruces	NM	254	289	-35.00
Stephen F. Austin State University	Nacodoches	TX	254	284	-30.00
Grambling State University	Grambling	LA	256	469	-213.00
Regis University	Denver	CO	257	76	181.00
University of North Carolina at Charlotte	Charlotte	NC	258	336	-78.00
Rochester Institute of Technology	Rochester	NY	259	249	10.00
Florida Atlantic University	Boca Raton	FL	260	91	169.00
California State University, Fullerton	Fullerton	CA	261	216	45.00
University of Toledo	Toledo	OH	262	224	38.00
Syracuse University	Syracuse	NY	263	403	-140.00
University of Massachusetts, Lowell	Lowell	MA	263	263	.00
Saint Joseph's University	Philadelphia	PA	265	438	-173.00
Stanford University	Stanford	CA	265	325	-60.00
Saint John's University	Jamaica	NY	265	28	237.00
Santa Clara University	Santa Clara	CA	268	131	137.00
Texas Woman's University	Denton	TX	269	159	110.00
Drake University	Des Moines	IA	270	446	-176.00
California State University, Northridge	Northridge	CA	271	301	-30.00
Western Michigan University	Kalamazoo	MI	272	253	19.00
University of Wisconsin, Madison	Madison	WI	273	125	148.00
Winthrop University	Rock Hill	SC	274	332	-58.00

School Name	City	State	APB	Chronicle	Difference
Northwestern University	Evanston	IL	274	255	19.00
Ohio State University	Columbus	OH	276	348	-72.00
Suffolk University	Boston	MA	276	83	193.00
Bradley University	Peoria	IL	278	354	-76.00
Lamar University	Beaumont	TX	279	442	-163.00
Southeastern Louisiana University	Hammond	LA	279	110	169.00
Duke University	Durham	NC	281	461	-180.00
University of Arkansas, Little Rock	Little Rock	AR	282	174	108.00
University of North Texas	Denton	TX	282	75	207.00
University of California, Los Angeles	Los Angeles	CA	284	407	-123.00
Eastern Michigan University	Ypsilanti	MI	285	383	-98.00
Georgia Southern University	Statesboro	GA	285	39	246.00
University of Saint Thomas	St. Paul	MN	287	381	-94.00
Southwest Texas State University	San Marcos	TX	288	152	136.00
University of Alabama at Huntsville	Huntsville	AL	289	333	-44.00
Rutgers University, New Brunswick	N. Brunswick	NJ	290	349	-59.00
Texas A&M University	College Station	TX	291	68	223.00
Our Lady of Holy Cross College	New Orleans	LA	292	184	108.00
University of Rochester	Rochester	NY	293	398	-105.00
Columbus State University	Columbus	GA	293	1	292.00
University of Dayton	Dayton	OH	295	432	-137.00
Central Connecticut State University	New Britain	CT	295	113	182.00
Rhode Island College	Providence	RI	297	1	296.00
Hofstra University	Hempstead	NY	298	147	151.00
Auburn University	Auburn	AL	299	87	212.00
Towson University	Towson	MD	300	236	64.00
Texas Christian University	Fort Worth	TX	301	148	153.00
University of San Francisco	San Francisco	CA	302	128	174.00
University of NC, Wilmington	Wilmington	NC	303	304	-1.00
Creighton University	Omaha	NE	304	246	58.00
Metropolitan State University	St. Paul	MN	305	58	247.00
State University of New York at Albany	Albany	NY	306	213	93.00
San Francisco State University	San Francisco	CA	306	145	161.00
Brown University	Providence	RI	308	358	-50.00
University of New Mexico	Alburquerque	NM	309	406	-97.00

School Name	City	State	APB	Chronicle	Difference
California Polytechnic State University	San Luis Obispo	CA	310	64	246.00
University of Kentucky	Lexington	KY	311	450	-139.00
University of California, Riverside	Riverside	CA	312	452	-140.00
University of Maryland, College Park	College Park	MD	312	400	-88.00
University of Texas, Austin	Austin	TX	312	129	183.00
Portland State University	Portland	OR	315	346	-31.00
Indiana Univ. -Purdue Univ., Indianapolis	Indianapolis	IN	316	80	236.00
Wake Forest University	Winston-Salem	NC	317	379	-62.00
College of Notre Dame of Maryland	Baltimore	MD	318	208	110.00
William Paterson University of New Jersey	Wayne	NJ	318	172	146.00
University of Denver	Denver	CO	318	117	201.00
Loyola College in Maryland	Baltimore	MD	321	123	198.00
The College of New Jersey	Ewing	NJ	322	157	165.00
California State University, Los Angeles	Los Angeles	CA	323	289	34.00
Johnson and Wales University	Providence	RI	324	369	-45.00
Texas A&M University, Kingsville	Kingsville	TX	325	47	278.00
University of Hawaii, Manoa	Honolulu	HI	326	305	21.00
La Salle University	Philadelphia	PA	327	458	-131.00
Northeastern Illinois University	Chicago	IL	328	227	101.00
Purdue University, Calumet	Hammond	IN	328	1	327.00
City University of NY, York College	Jamaica	NY	330	85	245.00
State University of NY College at Buffalo	Buffalo	NY	331	162	169.00
California State University, San Bernadino	S. Bernardino	CA	332	151	181.00
University of Georgia	Athens	GA	333	195	138.00
University of NC, Greensboro	Greensboro	NC	334	447	-113.00
Northern Arizona University	Flagstaff	AZ	335	389	-54.00
University of New Haven	West Haven	CT	335	202	133.00
Northwestern State Univ. of Louisiana	Natchitoches	LA	337	116	221.00
University of the District of Columbia	Washington	DC	338	70	268.00
San Jose State University	San Jose	CA	339	312	27.00
University of Miami	Coral Gables	FL	340	345	-5.00
Boston College	Chestnut Hill	MA	341	299	42.00
Arizona State University, Main	Tempe	AZ	342	374	-32.00
Hawaii Pacific University	Honolulu	HI	343	93	250.00
Baylor University	Waco	TX	343	65	278.00

School Name	City	State	APB	Chronicle	Difference
Xavier University	Cincinnati	OH	345	118	227.00
University of Nevada, Reno	Reno	NV	346	363	-17.00
Catholic University of America	Washington	DC	347	404	-57.00
Massachusetts Institute of Technology	Cambridge	MA	348	405	-57.00
University of Michigan, Dearborn	Dearborn	MI	349	65	284.00
NC Agricultural & Technical State Univ.	Greensboro	NC	350	467	-117.00
City University of NY, Brooklyn College	Brooklyn	NY	350	25	325.00
Valdosta State University	Valdosta	GA	352	234	118.00
City University of NY, Medgar Evers College	Brooklyn	NY	353	236	117.00
University of California, Berkeley	Berkeley	CA	354	436	-82.00
University of Texas, El Paso	El Paso	TX	355	135	220.00
University of Minnesota, Twin Cities	Minneapolis	MN	356	268	88.00
Wichita State University	Wichita	KS	357	98	259.00
Boston University	Boston	MA	358	339	19.00
University of South Carolina at Columbia	Columbia	SC	359	203	156.00
University of Massachusetts, Boston	Boston	MA	359	43	316.00
North Carolina Central University	Durham	NC	361	463	-102.00
Jersey City State College	Jersey City	NJ	362	154	208.00
University of Washington	Seattle	WA	362	118	244.00
University of Tennessee, Chattanooga	Chattanooga	TN	364	415	-51.00
California State University, Fresno	Fresno	CA	365	392	-27.00
City University of NY, Herbert H. Lehman College	Bronx	NY	365	88	277.00
University of South Florida	Tampa	FL	367	288	79.00
University of Missouri, Kansas City	Kansas City	MO	367	102	265.00
University of Southwestern Louisiana	Lafayette	LA	369	176	193.00
California State University, Dominguez Hills	Carson	CA	370	59	311.00
City University of NY, Hunter College	New York	NY	370	28	342.00
University of Nevada, Las Vegas	Las Vegas	NV	372	231	141.00
Barry University	Miami Shores	FL	373	78	295.00
University of South Alabama	Mobile	AL	374	238	136.00
California State University, Long Beach	Long Beach	CA	375	222	153.00
Widener University	Chester	PA	376	451	-75.00
Johns Hopkins University	Baltimore	MD	376	132	244.00

School Name	City	State	APB	Chronicle	Difference
University of the Pacific	Stockton	CA	378	377	1.00
Augusta State University	Augusta	GA	379	54	325.00
University of Alabama	Tuscaloosa	AL	380	249	131.00
University of Florida	Gainesville	FL	381	350	31.00
Southern Connecticut State University	New Haven	CT	382	160	222.00
College of Charleston	Charleston	SC	383	233	150.00
University of Southern Mississippi	Hattiesburg	MS	384	92	292.00
Florida International University	Miami	FL	385	275	110.00
University of Wisconsin, Milwaukee	Milwaukee	WI	385	112	273.00
University of Missouri, St. Louis	St. Louis	MO	387	98	289.00
Northeastern University	Boston	MA	388	274	114.00
Yale University	New Haven	CT	389	417	-28.00
Southern Methodist University	Dallas	TX	390	164	226.00
East Carolina University	Greenville	NC	391	397	-6.00
Albertus Magnus College	New Haven	CT	392	291	101.00
San Diego State University	San Diego	CA	392	118	274.00
Georgetown University	Washington	DC	394	164	230.00
University of Houston, Downtown	Houston	TX	395	273	122.00
Fordham University	Bronx	NY	396	114	282.00
Virginia Commonwealth University	Richmond	VA	397	278	119.00
Chicago State University	Chicago	IL	398	217	181.00
Alabama State University	Montgomery	AL	399	347	52.00
Old Dominion University	Norfolk	VA	400	344	56.00
City University of NY, John Jay College of Criminal Justice	New York	NY	401	27	374.00
Marquette University	Milwaukee	WI	402	371	31.00
Vanderbilt University	Nashville	TN	403	401	2.00
Thomas Edison State University	Trenton	NJ	404	1	403.00
Mercer University	Macon	GA	405	40	365.00
Tennessee State University	Nashville	TN	406	335	71.00
Embry-Riddle Aeronautical University	Daytona Beach	FL	407	1	406.00
University of Texas, Pan American	Edinburgh	TX	408	266	142.00
Kean University	Union	NJ	409	366	43.00
Nova Southeastern University	Fort Lauderdale	FL	410	1	409.00
City University of NY, NYC Tech College	Brooklyn	NY	411	225	186.00
University of Hartford	West Hartford	CT	412	355	57.00

School Name	City	State	APB	Chronicle	Difference
Carnegie Mellon University	Pittsburgh	PA	413	394	19.00
University of Maryland, Baltimore County	Baltimore	MD	414	210	204.00
North Carolina State University	Raleigh	NC	415	293	122.00
University of Alabama, Birmingham	Birmingham	AL	416	314	102.00
University of Pittsburgh	Pittsburgh	PA	417	402	15.00
Duquesne University	Pittsburgh	PA	418	281	137.00
University of New Orleans	New Orleans	LA	419	148	271.00
Howard University	Washington	DC	420	468	-48.00
Washington University	St. Louis	MO	420	182	238.00
Emory University	Atlanta	GA	422	443	-21.00
New York University	New York	NY	423	101	322.00
University of Louisville	Louisville	KY	424	322	102.00
Seattle University	Seattle	WA	425	48	377.00
Seton Hall University	South Orange	NJ	426	187	239.00
City University of NY, Baruch College	New York	NY	427	34	393.00
Troy State University, Montgomery	Montgomery	AL	428	168	260.00
Pace University	New York	NY	428	50	378.00
Indiana University Northwest	Gary	IN	430	342	88.00
Roosevelt University	Chicago	IL	431	41	390.00
Long Island University, Brooklyn Campus	Brooklyn	NY	431	1	430.00
Golden Gate University	San Francisco	CA	433	1	432.00
University of Memphis	Memphis	TN	434	180	254.00
Florida State University	Tallahassee	FL	435	306	129.00
University of Southern California	Los Angeles	CA	436	456	-20.00
University of Detroit, Mercy	Detroit	MI	437	263	174.00
University of Cincinnati	Cincinnati	OH	438	323	115.00
Yeshiva University	New York	NY	439	1	438.00
Barnard College, Columbia University	New York	NY	440	34	406.00
Loyola University of Chicago, Water Tower	Chicago	IL	441	173	268.00
Norfolk State University	Norfolk	VA	442	413	29.00
Drexel University	Philadelphia	PA	443	459	-16.00
George Washington University	Washington	DC	444	331	113.00
Case Western Reserve University	Cleveland	OH	445	318	127.00
Tulane University	New Orleans	LA	446	391	55.00
Rutgers University, Newark	Newark	NJ	446	281	165.00

School Name	City	State	APB	Chronicle	Difference
Columbia University, School of General Studies	New York	NY	448	419	29.00
Columbia University, Engineering and Applied Sciences	New York	NY	448	419	29.00
Columbia University, Columbia College	New York	NY	448	419	29.00
University of Pennsylvania	Philadelphia	PA	451	449	2.00
Wayne State University	Detroit	MI	452	256	196.00
Cleveland State University	Cleveland	OH	453	230	223.00
Jackson State University	Jackson	MS	454	448	6.00
New Jersey Institute of Technology	Newark	NJ	455	318	137.00
DePaul University, Chicago Loop Campus	Chicago	IL	456	186	270.00
Columbia College, Chicago	Chicago	IL	457	30	427.00
University of Chicago	Chicago	IL	458	380	78.00
Northeast Louisiana University	Monroe	LA	459	280	179.00
University of Houston	Houston	TX	460	135	325.00
University of Illinois at Chicago	Chicago	IL	461	193	268.00
Saint Louis University	St. Louis	MO	462	209	253.00
Georgia Institute of Technology	Atlanta	GA	463	412	51.00
Georgia State University	Atlanta	GA	464	248	216.00
Texas Southern University	Houston	TX	465	465	.00
Temple University	Philadelphia	PA	466	267	199.00
Illinois Institute of Technology	Chicago	IL	467	269	198.00
Southern University and A&M College	Baton Rouge	LA	468	326	142.00
City University of NY, City College	New York	NY	469	225	244.00
Clark Atlanta University	Atlanta	GA	470	433	37.00

CHAPTER III.
CAMPUS POLICING

In this chapter we examine Pearson and Toby's (1991) third risk factor: the hypothesized lack of formal security on college campuses. Even if this were true in the past, it is not likely to be the case on most contemporary campuses. Campus administrators realize that even a single highly publicized crime can seriously affect their ability to attract students.

Fox and Hellman (1985) suggest that one reason that urban schools do not have higher total crime rates than their suburban and rural counterparts may be due to the low crime rates at urban commuter schools. They also argue that urban campus administrators protect their campuses more, thereby reducing the impact of, or crime spillover from, the surrounding community (Hakim and Rengert, 1981). Their analysis of the strength of campus police forces by location discovered that, for the most part, location was unimportant. Fox and Hellman (1985:441) note:

> There is light evidence that in the larger metropolitan areas, campuses protect themselves a bit more. Generally, however, urban campuses do not protect themselves more than suburban or rural campuses... Finally, the intuition-contradicting finding that higher levels of police enforcement are associated with higher, not lower, rates of campus crime may simply reflect an unresolved simultaneity bias. That is: the simple correlation between campus crime rates and campus police strength confounds two opposite effects: campuses with large police forces presumably prevent crime on campus and campuses with severe crime problems enlist additional police in an attempt to combat the crime problem.

Research findings are not consistent on the relationship between the number of security personnel and campus victimization. In contrast to Fox and Hellman (1985), a recent study by Fisher et al. (1998) found the number of campus security personnel was unrelated to victimization rates on campus.

The History of Campus Security

In order to understand the complexity of campus security and safety, it is instructive to trace its development historically to determine how it evolved into its present form. Although campus security functions have existed nearly as long as there have been campuses, campus police functions are relatively young and continue to evolve. We will divide the development of campus police functions into four stages, beginning with the colonial period.

The beginning of the campus police force can be traced back to colonial times, when it was part of the maintenance staff. This stage lasted from the early 1700s through 1919. The primary concern was the protection of campus property through fire prevention, waste disposal, and the control of trespassers and stray animals on campus (Nichols, 1987). This primarily was a security force since campuses were generally separated from the surrounding community and interaction with the surrounding community was not considered important. The faculty and administrators of the campus controlled student conduct according to the principle of *in loco parentis*. This meant that the campus faculty and administrators would act much like (or in place of) parents in controlling student conduct. They would have broad powers and could act in an authoritative manner to address student misbehavior.

The campus was considered a closed community immune from outside influences. The fortunate few were admitted as students and their behavior was tightly controlled by a hierarchical system of campus administrators, faculty and older students. Some military colleges have maintained this tight hierarchical structure to this day. The direct provision of security was in the hands of the janitor and/or the watchman. Toward the end of this period, the embryonic beginning of a campus police force designed to protect students as well as campus property took place. Yale University established a small two-person police force in 1894 to protect students from townspeople. The first two officers were recruited from the New Haven police officers corps (Nichols, 1987). However, Yale was very unusual. Most campuses did not have formal police departments during this period. There was little need for a formal campus police force because local police handled any criminal violations, while the faculty handled minor infractions and misbehavior.

The second stage, beginning in the 1920s and continuing through the 1950s, was characterized by the watchman or guard model. These watchmen were commonly employed when the campus was the least active — at night and on the weekends. These employees were commonly older, retired individuals whose main responsibility was the protection of campus property. They differed from their predecessors in that they focused entirely on security, rather than combining it with janitorial and maintenance functions. Still, they were commonly housed in the maintenance or the physical plant department of the campus (Nichols, 1987).

Although they were hired to protect campus property, these watchmen were neither expected to nor capable of engaging in law enforcement functions. Their primary function was prevention, not enforcement. The watchmen maintained the security of buildings and their contents by ensuring that doors and windows were locked, pipes did not leak, and fire hazards did not exist. When open consumption of alcohol returned to campus with the repeal of Prohibition in the early 1930s, the watchman-guard gradually began to take on a broader role of rule enforcer to control the conduct of those who were drinking (Bordner and Petersen, 1983). The watchmen slowly began to assume the role that in the previous era was reserved to local police or campus faculty. Their concern was not only the prevention of crime, but also the control of conduct and the apprehension of misbehaving students.

During this stage, additional universities began to establish campus police departments. In one case, a department evolved from local police being assigned campus-policing duties on a rotating basis. At the University of Maryland in 1936, two Maryland State Troopers who had been on temporary assignment to campus duty volunteered for permanent assignment to the campus. They were subsequently hired by the university as campus police officers (Sides, 1983).

The complexity of campus security began to increase following World War II. The GI Bill allowed returning veterans of the war to attain a higher education, and many took advantage of the opportunity. Enrollments expanded greatly and the characteristics of students became much more diverse, not only in age, but also in socioeconomic background.

Campus administrators began to recognize the need for a more organized policing function. Problems resulted not only from increased enrollments, but also from expansion in the physical size of the campus, the legalization of alcohol, the increase in female enrollment and concern for the safety of female students. Campuses became more open to the surrounding community through community programming, cultural events and sports. More students brought cars onto campus, creating new traffic and parking problems. Finally, a more diverse student body seeking greater autonomy called for a more sophisticated approach to campus safety and security issues. The watchman-guard of this stage began to evolve into a more professionally trained and professionally oriented police officer.

Stage three, from the 1960s through the 1970s, was the era of campus unrest and security breakdown. Several factors converged at this stage to dramatically change the image and function of campus safety and security. One of the most important factors affecting campus security was the demise of *in loco parentis*. Throughout the first half of this century, colleges and universities relied on the authority given to them through *in loco parentis* to discipline their students. The legal doctrine gives a non-parent authority over another person, and under this doctrine institutions governed their students as parents would a child. In the 1960s, students rebelled against the doctrine. Returning military veterans often resented the strict disciplinary rules, while other students began to question campus and political authority. Students wished to be treated as adults rather than children by campus administrators, while campus administrators held tightly to their "parental" roles. These opposing forces led to legal battles. While *in loco parentis* has never been overruled, the doctrine has been deemphasized. Court cases such as Dixon v. the Alabama Board of Education — which held in 1961 that a university could not discipline students without providing them due process — led universities to reduce the amount of control they exercised over students. This case began the process of gradual change in which campus administrators began to give students greater autonomy. Curfews began to be abolished, students were allowed to live off campus and coed dorms were established. In short, students became responsible for governing their own behavior, and campus administrators and faculty became less responsible for governing student behavior. Campus administrators found themselves caught between conflicting forces. On the one hand, the courts ruled that colleges must afford students the same rights and privileges as any other citizen. On the other hand, campus administrators were responsible and liable for the safety and welfare of the students. A fine balance was required to reconcile these forces.

The second factor to occur in this stage was the Vietnam War and draft exemptions for college students. Some young men who had little interest in a college education found themselves in college to avoid being drafted into the Vietnam War. Individuals attending college who had little interest in education presented a new problem to campus administrators. These students did not hesitate to disrupt the traditional educational mission of the campus for political causes or personal amusement. Many campuses experienced disruptions as these students and their followers organized demonstrations, occupied buildings and destroyed property. The watchman/guards were ill prepared to confront this human element of campus security and safety. Most had been trained in law enforcement agencies that were not overly concerned with the civil liberties of criminals, only their apprehension. Campus administrators became dissatisfied with the training of these officers as well as the assistance rendered by outside agencies when campus unrest occurred (e.g., the Ohio National Guard at Kent State University).

The final factor that converged during this time period was the rise of racial and sexual liberation movements. Before this period, segregated all-male, all-female and all-black colleges were common. Furthermore, white male students made up the majority of the campus population. This began to change in a radical manner in the 1960s. Today, the number of female students commonly exceeds the number of males in large state universities. Black students now attend universities to which they were previously denied admission. Clearly, increased diversity allows a richer educational experience. However, it also creates increased demands on campus safety officers, who must be concerned with gender and hate crimes on campus.

Campus administrators began to recognize that they required something more than was being provided by officers trained within local and state police departments (Nichols, 1987). Rather than being trained to solve crimes, they required personnel trained in human relations so as to defuse volatile confrontations and to create a campus climate within which students like and respect campus police personnel. Students choose a college partly because they want to live there, and they do not want to live where they fear the local police officers. This reorientation lead to stage four of campus security evolution. The emphasis changed from law enforcement to community policing, with officers now concerned with the human element of problem solving rather than the technical elements of crime fighting. The concept of hiring former local police officers lost its popularity. Campuses began to train their own public safety personnel (Nichols, 1997).

Stage four roughly extends from the 1980s to the present. In this stage, campus police have changed their role from property protection to more professional policing with a human orientation. Also, student enrollments began to decline in the 1980s and early 1990s and campus administrators became concerned with student recruitment, retention and the financial viability of their institutions. All of these factors are interrelated. Feeling safe on campus affects the overall quality of life and the educational progress of students. Students choose an institution of higher education that they perceive offers these qualities. A well publicized crime not only affects student enrollment and retention, it also can lead to civil court proceedings and dollar damages collected by victims or their relatives. These legal proceedings also may be publicized, leading to a protracted period in which the reputation of a college or university is soiled. Campus administrators wish to avoid these circumstances at all costs.

Campus safety also affects the productivity of faculty and staff who work on campus. Faculty who leave campus before dark for fear of crime, instead of staying late to finish a research project or prepare a lecture, are compromising the quality of their work for the feeling of safety. If widespread, the quality of faculty and staff output on campus will be lower than on a campus where faculty and staff feel safe and secure working late into the night.

Finally, parents, who usually pay the bills, demand that the campus be safe. In short, the perceived safety and security of a campus is integrally intertwined with the fiscal health of the institution. Also important is the threat of a lawsuit if campus security is deemed to be lax. One might even term this stage the "liability awareness stage."

Liability Awareness and Campus Policing

This heightened emphasis on safety requires a reorientation of the manner in which policing is carried out on campus compared to the surrounding community. Traditional policing in the surrounding community often focuses on apprehending criminals rather than preventing crime. However, on a college campus, once a crime is committed, the damage has already been done and apprehending the criminal does little to repair it. Rather, the goal of campus police officers as well as their administrators must be on keeping the crime from occurring in the first place. There are two facets of this approach we can identify in the literature, community-oriented policing (Goldstein, 1990) and situational crime control (Clarke, 1992).

Community-oriented or problem-solving policing focuses on the human element. The objective is to work closely with the campus community to identify potential problems before they escalate into crimes or disorder. Campus police personnel interact closely with students and faculty so that they recognize potential conflict or concerns that can cause security or safety problems. Examples include quelling racial unrest before it escalates into a disturbance or a hate crime; securing a secluded area on campus where students gather to experiment with illegal drugs before a student dies of a drug overdose; or, identifying a rowdy fraternity that has uncontrolled parties before a female student is raped or a student dies of alcohol poisoning. Knowledge of these circumstances requires campus police personnel to have an ear for potential problems and a positive relationship with students and faculty.

Interaction with the campus community is critical. For example, in the 1980s, San Francisco Community College failed to disclose a series of rapes that occurred in a university parking lot. Because the public was not warned of the potential danger, the college was successfully sued by a victim of attempted rape in that same parking lot (Peterson v. San Francisco Community College District, 1984). The court held that universities have a duty to inform students of safety hazards that they know exist on or near campus. Carrying out this duty to inform requires communication between students, faculty and campus police.

The second means by which campus police can prevent crime before it occurs is through situational crime control. This involves identifying criminogenic environments and changing them before a crime takes place. It relies upon a variety of environmental design and management measures to increase the difficulty and risks of committing crime (Clarke and Mayhew, 1980). This is a very practical approach.

Clarke (1988:4) points out that practitioners responsible for security frequently complain that criminological theories are too abstract to be of value in their day-to-day work. Most theories have sought to explain delinquency by factors such as poverty, broken homes, personality deficiencies, poor schooling, unequal opportunities and discrimination. These are matters largely outside the province of security practitioners, who have to take society as given. Their primary concern is the security of their employers' property and interests. Most of their preventive efforts can be described in one short phrase: reducing opportunities for crime.

One aspect of this approach is Crime Prevention Through Environmental Design (CPTED). This involves not only the architecture of buildings and landscape architecture of grounds, but also lighting, sight lines, and defensible spaces allocated to specific functions rather than ambiguous in their purpose (Newman, 1972). For example, Fisher (1998:115) advocates that "…architects of a proposed new building should be required to detail who will use the facility, when, and for what purposes, and to describe how users' activities may create opportunities for victimization and fear." Landscaping should be trimmed to no more than 18 inches. Sight lines should be maintained to avoid blind spots and obstructed views. Finally, since most perpetrators of campus crime come from the student population, fencing off the campus may have limited benefits; one must consider whether you are fencing perpetrators out or fencing them in.

Another aspect of situational crime control is target-hardening. In this instance, campus police use technology to make committing a crime more difficult or the probability of detection more likely. For example, campus police may install a closed-circuit television camera near a vending machine that has been vandalized on numerous occasions. Once an offender is caught on camera, others are likely to avoid this target. Another means of target-hardening is to station a police officer in a particularly vulnerable location at a particularly vulnerable time. A simple example is the assignment of police personnel to sporting events, where alcohol consumption and rival fans may create security problems. A final example is a public transportation station where students and faculty await a carrier. In off-hours, these people are potential targets for personal crime such as rape or robbery. Stationing a police officer near this location may prevent a crime from occurring.

Finally, newly developed computer software allows police administrators to identify clusters of crime in space and time. This technology also allows administrators to monitor the success of remedial actions. Most of these techniques are based on Geographic Information Systems (GIS), the use of which has spread through police departments since the late 1980s and throughout the 1990s. The best known is the ComStat program of the New York City Police Department. This program seeks to identify concentrations of crime termed "hot spots" and to hold police administrators responsible for effective solutions. In other words, rather than waiting for a crime to occur and responding to it, the commanders are responsible for developing ideas to deter future crime. GIS monitors success in deterring crime. The importance of Geographic Information Systems to policing cannot be overestimated. Today, about 13% of law enforcement agencies are using GIS regularly to analyze crime problems in their jurisdictions (Harries, 1999). In the near future, a majority will do so.

Traditional GIS is less useful for campus police because it ignores important features of college campuses that may be related to crime. For example, it is common for a campus building to be a block long and many stories high. Allocating all crime in the building to a single address does not tell a campus police administrator much of what he or she needs to know. In Appendix 1, we outline the development of high-definition GIS and illustrate its usefulness to campus police as well as other police agencies responsible for spatially compact areas. Shopping mall security, public housing police and security in the central business districts of major cities are just three other examples of security agencies responsible for relatively small areas containing multistoried structures that can profitably use high-definition GIS.

CHAPTER IV.
SITUATIONAL CRIME CONTROL USING HIGH-DEFINITION GIS

Between 1960 and 1990, the number of students pursuing higher education in the United States increased from 4 million to approximately 14 million. The number of institutions of higher education increased from about 2,000 to more than three and a half thousand (United States Department of Education, 1991). Yet, very little research has focused on the special problems of campus police.

Furthermore, some of the best developments in the research of spatial patterns of crime do not apply to the campus situation. For example, the technique of "geographic profiling" recently developed by Rossmo (1995) is designed to predict the home or work place of an offender by the spatial pattern of their offenses. The technique is based on a distance-minimization routine of the point pattern of crimes. Such distance-based measures have less meaning in a campus environment, where it is estimated that 80% to 90% of the crimes are committed by students (Smith and Smith, 1990). If the students live on campus, the spatial pattern of campus offenses is not likely to provide clues — beyond simple cases such as vandalism on the floor where a delinquent student resides. Even commuting students are attracted to campus for reasons other than crime, and therefore the spatial pattern of crime committed by a single student is not likely to provide clues to where this student resides. More meaningful for a campus environment is controlling crime through community cooperation using situational means of crime control. This entails explicitly locating the criminogenic environments on campus, and, in consultation with the campus community, determining which remedial efforts are most likely to be successful in removing the localized opportunities for crime. Clarke (1992) terms such remedial efforts situational crime control.

High-definition Geographic Information Systems (GIS) allow more meaningful analysis of situational crime control. Such variables as lighting, controlled access to buildings, and landscaping can be identified and evaluated more directly than in a traditional, address-based GIS. For example, address-based GIS might tell us that there is a hot spot of crime in the campus recreation building. A high-definition GIS might tell us that this hot spot of crime is contained in the public locker area of the campus recreation building, indicating that situational crime control efforts would be more effective focusing on improved locker security rather than tightening security in areas of the building not affected by crime. In other words, the microenvironment so critical to understanding environmental criminology can be examined directly in a high-definition GIS.

Situational Elements Associated with Crime Patterns on Temple's Campus

The following discussion examines the use of high-definition GIS to identify and evaluate situational means of crime control. Three topological components of GIS are used: points, lines and polygons. We begin with an examination of point features that influence crime patterns.

Point Features

Point features of the environment are very small unique features that do not have an important spatial extent and do not usually reoccur in a uniform spatial pattern. Rather, they exist at defined locations and can act either as an attraction to criminals (such as an automatic teller machine), or a repellant to criminal activity (such as a police kiosk). Analyzing crime patterns around a point feature in space becomes problematic when crime is a rare event. When examining point features, it is likely that any one feature will not have enough crime associated with it to identify a pattern. However, GIS allows us to solve this problem by aggregating the data surrounding several similar point features so that enough crimes are present to identify a pattern.

Police Kiosks

An example of a point feature on Temple University's campus that was explicitly designed to deter criminal activity is a police kiosk (see Figure 3).

Temple University constructed three police kiosks with the express purpose of protecting especially important walkways from crime. The first was constructed in 1995 at the commuter train station. The next was constructed in 1997 at the campus end of the walkway to the commuter train station. This walkway is about two blocks in length and passes through the community surrounding Temple's campus. The third kiosk was built in 1998 on the opposite side of the campus, to secure pathways to athletic facilities.

High-definition GIS is well suited to test whether these kiosks have effectively served their purpose. If effective, we would expect crimes to decrease following their construction in the areas closest to the kiosks. We began by defining the security kiosks as point features in our high-definition GIS. Then, we divided the distance between the two kiosks protecting the walkway from the campus to the train station into two equal parts. We created a buffer around each kiosk, using that distance as the buffer radius. Finally, we divided each buffer into two equal parts composed of an inner circle and outer circle. Street robberies were plotted in these buffers. This process enabled us to observe the spatial and temporal arrangement of crime surrounding the security kiosks. Again, we expected crime in the circles to decrease after construction of the police kiosks. And we were able to observe whether crime was spatially displaced from the inner circle to the outer circle following the construction of the security kiosks. We have the richest data from the train station kiosk since it was the first to be built (see Figure 4). As can be seen, this kiosk was built in a very criminogenic environment under a railroad overpass next to abandoned factory buildings on the right of the kiosk. It also is adjacent to public housing to the left of the kiosk. In short, it is in a relatively dark insecure location.

We compared the five years before the kiosk was built with the three years after it was built using both total figures and figures for each circle. The average number of street crimes per year for both rings for the five years before the kiosk was built is 11. The average figure for the three years after the kiosk was built is 2.6 crimes per year. Clearly, this police kiosk seems to have fulfilled its function of reducing crime in its half of the walkway from the main campus.

Figure 3: Temple University Police Kiosks

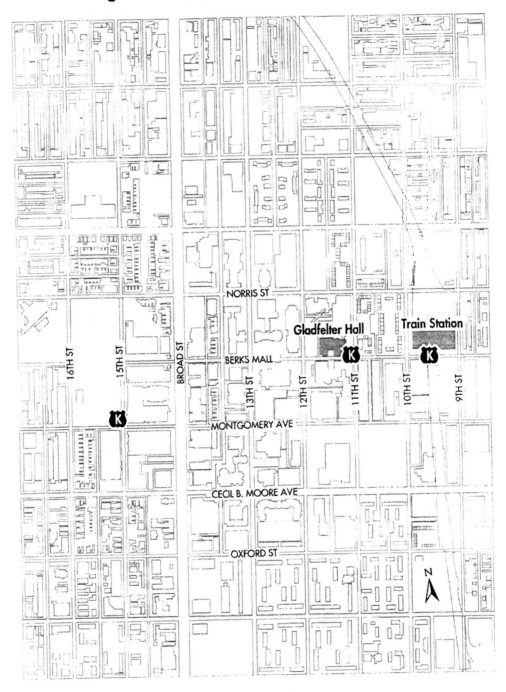

Figure 4: Train Station Security Kiosk

A comparison of crime in the inner and outer circles provided further evidence of the kiosk's effectiveness. Crime decreased more in the inner circle surrounding the security kiosk than in the outer circle that is at the limits of its control. The inner circle contained an average of 10.4 crimes per year before the kiosk was built and an average of 2 crimes per year after the kiosk was built. This is a decrease of about 81%. The outside buffer contained an average of 0.6 crimes per year before the kiosk was constructed and 0.6 crimes per year after it was constructed. Clearly, the train station attracted criminals to its environs, and, after the kiosk was built it deterred this crime with no evidence of spatial displacement to the outer circle. Furthermore, the figures are nearly the same if the circles are constructed to contain equal area (see Figure 5) or to have an equal radius.

Figure 5: Train Station Security Kiosk with Buffers

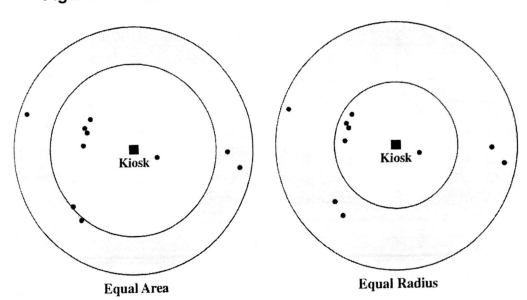

Equal Area   Equal Radius

In order to obtain more data on the effectiveness of police kiosks, we aggregated the two kiosks between the commuter train station and Gladfelter Hall. Data are displayed by overlaying the areas surrounding each kiosk (see Figure 6). This provides more data points than if each kiosk were considered separately. This is an important utility of high-definition GIS. Since crime is a rare event, aggregation of like environmental features is often necessary to discover spatial or temporal patterns. The overlaying capability of GIS allows the aggregation necessary to highlight spatial and temporal patterns about point features in space.

Figure 6: Temple University Police Kiosks, Aggregated Data 1991 through 1998

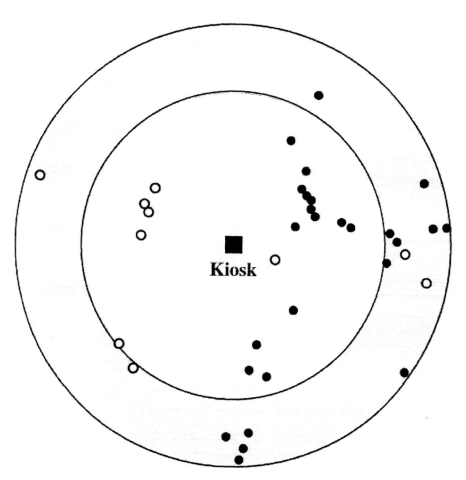

● Crimes around the Gladfelter Hall security kiosk

○ Crimes around the train station security kiosk

■ Security kiosk

Our analysis illustrates that before the construction of each kiosk, the inner circle experienced 83 crimes and the outer buffer experienced 36 crimes. In other words, the inner circle, which is the same size as the outer circle, experienced 2.3 times as many crimes. After the kiosks were constructed, the inner circle experienced 7 crimes and the outer circle experienced 3 crimes. This also is 2.3 times as many crimes in the inner circle as the outer circle. Therefore, there is no evidence of spatial displacement of crime from the inner circles to the outer circles. Most important, there is clear evidence that crime has been reduced due to the construction of the police kiosks (see Figure 7).

Figure 7: Impact of Security Kiosks on Crime

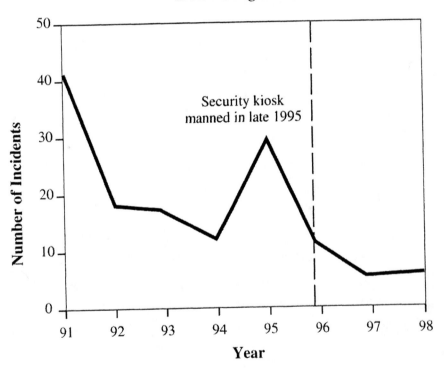

**All Outside Crime Occurring
within Security Kiosk Buffers
1991 through 1998**

Situational analysis of point features in space would also be useful for Automatic Teller Machines (ATM). However, all of these machines are contained within buildings on Temple University's campus. As such, they are only available when buildings are unlocked during business hours. They are well protected and do not attract criminals. Other examples of point features that could be analyzed by high-definition GIS include security stations at the entrances to public housing or campus dormitories, sales booths at sporting events or movie theaters in city center districts. Any feature that is essentially a point on a map, especially on a high-definition GIS map can be analyzed as a point feature in GIS.

Line Features

Next, we will consider line features. Line features are generally considered barriers to spatial movement since they often depict boundaries between areas. Physical examples of line features in the larger environment are rivers and mountain ranges. Within an urban area, boundaries between social and ethnic groups are expected to influence interaction (Morrill, 1965; Pettiway, 1982). At the campus scale of analysis, one of the most important linear features is the campus boundary. It is not clear whether this boundary deters crime or attracts criminals from the outside. Part of the answer depends on the permeability of the boundary.

In previous analyses of whether a campus attracts or repels criminals, crime on campus was compared with the crime rate of the community within which it is situated (Fox and Hellman, 1985; Bromley, 1992). The problem with such analyses is that they ignore the spatial element with regard to the distance a criminal is likely to travel for purposes of crime (Capone and Nichols, 1976; Rengert and Wasilchick, 1985). For example, it is unlikely that a criminal living in South Philadelphia will travel all the way to Temple University, located in North Philadelphia, to commit a crime. Temple University is not likely to attract criminals from beyond the area they use on a routine basis (Rengert and Wasilchick, 1985). We must analyze a much smaller environment to test whether a campus attracts criminals from the outside. High-definition GIS allows us to accomplish this.

Temple University is an open university; it has no walls or fences separating it from the surrounding community. Its symbolic boundaries are easily crossed and not designed to deter spatial movement. However, it is clear when one passes from the surrounding community of row houses to the high-rise buildings of Temple University's campus. Fisher et al. (1998:701) state this issue clearly:

> ...the effects of wider contextual variables might be mitigated by the distinct boundaries that often separate college campuses from the community (e.g. gate houses, fences, hedges, and distinct buildings)... Campuses are likely to be places that potential offenders do not "habitually use" and thus are not well integrated into their cognitive maps... Travelling onto a campus to commit a crime — especially if offenders "stand out" socially — may prove too uncomfortable to be practiced regularly. In short, as geographically and socially distinct space, campuses may insulate themselves from the larger context by erecting both physical and social-psychological barriers to potential offenders.

We use high-definition GIS to determine whether the campus boundary has an effect on the pattern of crime.

Fernandez and Lizotte (1995) discovered that only robbery and motor vehicle theft in the surrounding community affected the rate of these crimes on campus. The pattern was not evident for other crimes. Therefore, these two crimes are well suited to evaluate any effect of the campus boundary on the spatial pattern of crime. Eleventh Street forms the eastern boundary of Temple University's campus proper (see Figure 8). We begin by evaluating the pattern of street robberies over a period of eight years (1991 through 1998) on each side of this line feature.

Street Robberies — Temple

High-definition GIS has the capability of creating "buffer zones" on each side of the line feature that is the campus boundary. We construct two buffers on either side of the boundary: the first is 460 feet in width (approximately one city block), the second an additional 460 feet in width. Attaching crime data to these buffers allows us to measure the impact of the campus boundary on crime. If the campus boundary deters criminals from the surrounding community, then we would expect crime to decrease in the two buffer regions inside the campus as compared to the two buffer regions out-

Figure 8: 11th Street Boundary

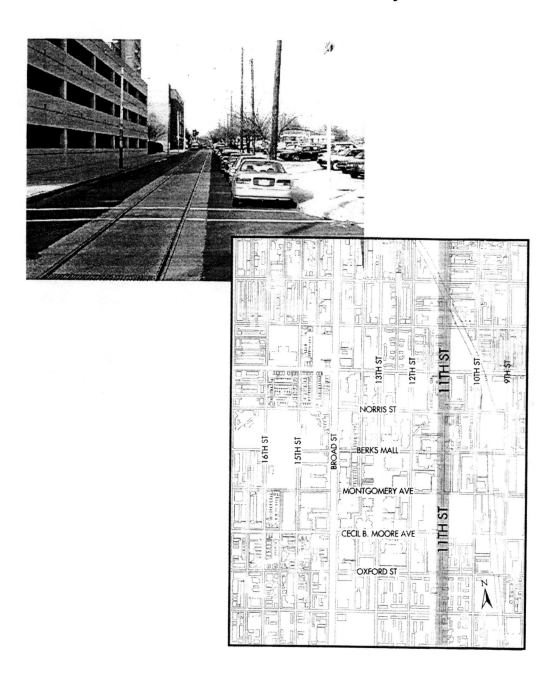

side the campus. If the campus attracts robbers and auto thieves from the surrounding community, as suggested by Fernandez and Lizotte (1995), crime should be higher on the campus side of the boundary. On the other hand, if most of this crime is committed by students (Smith and Smith, 1990), then we would expect crime to be higher on the campus side of the boundary and less in the surrounding community. An idea of whether these crimes are committed by residents of the surrounding community can be obtained by comparing the spatial pattern of crime of the buffers. If most of the crime is committed by residents of the surrounding community, Brantingham et al. (1995:134) provide us with the expected spatial pattern: "Crimes by outsiders are most likely to occur...on the edge of campus and in areas adjacent to the campus edge." In this case, we would expect the buffers on either side of the campus boundary to experience the most crime. On the other hand, if the buffer farthest inside the campus experienced the most crime, it is a sign the crime is not committed predominantly by residents of the surrounding community. There is no reason to believe criminals from the surrounding community will travel farther than necessary to identify an opportunity for crime within or around the campus.

In contrast, members of the campus community may feel more comfortable committing a crime in the heart of their campus. Again, Brantingham et al. (1995:134) address this issue: "The important point about the surroundings of a campus and the permeability of the campus border is that crime...may be generated by a mixture of insiders and outsiders or may be generated by situations created by insiders alone." The spatial arrangement of crime between the buffers provides clues to resolve this issue. We begin by measuring whether or not the campus boundary has an effect on the spatial pattern of crime. Then we will compare the amount of crime within each buffer to determine whether it is likely to have been committed by residents of the surrounding community.

The effect of the campus boundary can be measured by graphing the number of crimes occurring in each buffer zone on each side of the boundary. Then, a "least squares line" that best fits the four data points is constructed on the graph. Finally, the origin points of the lines on each side of the boundary are changed so that the "least squares line" best fits only the points on that side of the boundary. The vertical distance between the origin points of the lines at the boundary illustrates the impact of the boundary on campus crime. In the case of street robbery, it is clear that the campus either attracts criminals from the surrounding community or constrains the activities of campus criminals. In either case, the boundary is associated with an increase in street robberies by 25 crimes over the eight-year period on the campus side of the boundary (see Figure 9).

Evidence of whether the majority of these crimes was committed by residents of the surrounding community can be obtained by comparing the amount of crime within each buffer. In the present case, the buffer closest to the heart of the campus had the most crime. This implies that residents of the surrounding community were not likely to be responsible for the majority of this crime. This information is very important for campus administrators in formulating crime prevention strategies. Brantingham et al. (1995:134) make this point:

> Most people make the insider/outsider distinction. We want people who cause problems to look different from "us." Campus insiders seem to believe this though data indicate that most campus crimes are committed by campus insiders.

Crime prevention strategies focused on the campus community may be more fruitful in the case of street robberies.

If we analyze auto thefts and break-ins on either side of the campus boundary, we obtain similar results. Using both Temple University and Philadelphia police data, we examined crime in the two blocks on either side of 11th Street, and graphed the number of auto thefts and break-ins. In this case, the campus boundary was associated with an increase in these crimes of about 395 events over an eight-year period (see Figure 10).

Temple is largely a commuter campus that does not provide many opportunities for student victimization in the surrounding community. In an analysis of the use of the surrounding community by Temple students and faculty over a typical 24-hour period, these groups spent 87% of their time on campus and only 13% of their time in the surrounding community. Therefore, there is little opportunity for student victimization in the community surrounding Temple University. The situation will be very different in a predominantly residential community such as the University of Pennsylvania.

Figure 9: Effect of 11th Street Boundary on Street Robberies

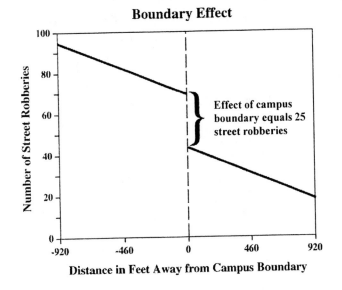

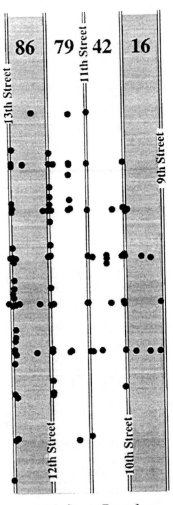

11th Street Boundary

Figure 10: Effect of 11th Street Boundary on Auto Theft, Break-ins and Vandalism

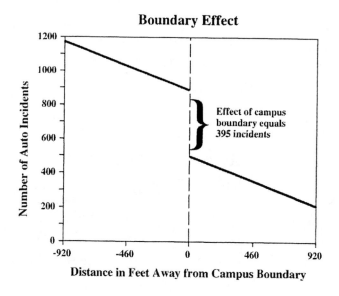

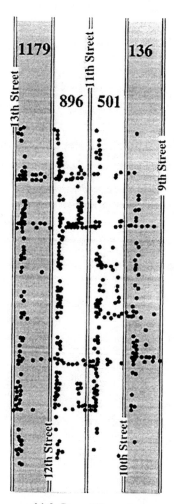

11th Street Boundary

Street Robberies – Penn

The effect of the campus boundary on street robbery at the University of Pennsylvania can be analyzed for 1995. Fortieth Street was designated as the western boundary of the campus, and street robbery was analyzed for two blocks on each side of this boundary. In this case, the campus boundary seemed to have no effect; the pattern of crime was curvilinear rather than linear as in the case of Temple University. Street robbery clearly clustered near this boundary, with the greatest amount on the first block into the surrounding community rather than on campus as in the example of Temple University (see Figure 11).

Students at The University of Pennsylvania use the surrounding community more than do students at Temple University. Many Penn students live in private apartments in the community, while almost none of the Temple students live in the surrounding community in private apartments. Therefore, Penn students provide more targets or opportunities for crime on the neighborhood side of the campus boundary than do students from a largely commuter campus. As noted on Figure 2, many of these robberies occur near a famous college bar (Smokey Joe's) that is patronized not only by students from the University of Pennsylvania, but also by students from throughout the region, including Temple students. There are about 15 street robberies in or near this bar in one year (located on the community side of the campus boundary). The campus boundary does not seem to deter criminals in this case. Rather, crime seems to be clustered near it. Using the reasoning of Brantingham et al. (1995), this pattern implies that a high proportion of the perpetrators come from the surrounding community.

The difference between these two campuses in Philadelphia contrasts important characteristics of a predominantly commuter campus and a predominantly residential campus. Both street robbery and auto theft are outdoor crimes. We turn our attention next to indoor crime and crime patterns in the vertical dimension. Here we examine polygon features using high-definition GIS.

Figure 11: University of Pennsylvania Street Robberies near 40th Street Campus Boundary

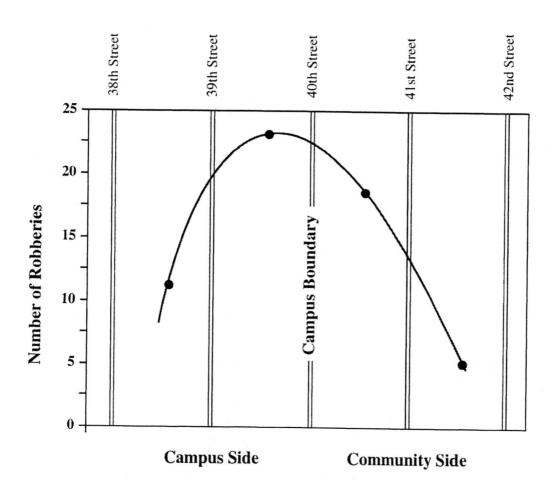

Polygon Features

Polygon features have areal extent in either two or three dimensions. A recent advancement in the identification of two-dimensional polygon features has been termed "hot-spot" policing (Block, 1994). Sherman and Weisburd (1995) evaluated this procedure and concluded that preventive patrol focused on micro-level hot spots is useful under certain circumstances. The premise on which the organization of patrol beats is set, where the entire beat must be consistently patrolled throughout a shift, may be misguided. In fact, police on random patrol may avoid areas where they are most needed (Herbert, 1997). If the locations where crime is highly concentrated can be identified, these areas should receive the bulk of police attention while on patrol. In an experiment to determine the effect of preventive patrol of this nature, Sherman and Weisburd (1995) doubled the "observed" patrol of half of the hot spots, which resulted in 6% to 13% decreases in calls for service in these advantaged spots compared to those where preventive patrol was not increased.

A serious problem associated with how "hot spots" of crime are identified has not been adequately addressed. To date, the vertical dimension of a crime hot spot has not been explicitly considered. For example, a ten-story building has ten times the horizontal space as the ground level "foot print" of the building. However, in most hot-spot analysis, this fact is ignored and crime is mapped in two dimensions. Often, all the crime of a multistory building is associated with the address of the building — as if it were a single point in space (Wilkins, 1996). To avoid falsely identifying hot spots, Sherman and Weisburd (1995) excluded locations such as hospitals, residential, and commercial buildings with more than three stories in height. However, much of the built environment of a modern campus, high-rise public housing estate or a center-city district would be excluded using this criteria. Campus security needs a geographic information system that will track the vertical as well as the horizontal dimension of crime patterns.

An example of the identification of a "false hot spot" of crime is contained in an analysis of auto theft in central Philadelphia. Rengert (1997) identified a hot spot of auto theft on South Street using the STAC program (Block, 1994) (see Figure 12, ellipse 10). Through his knowledge of South Street as an entertainment center of the city, Rengert ascribed the concentration of auto theft to a record store located in the hot spot that attracts customers from a wide area. However, when he examined the addresses about which the cars were stolen, he found that the vast majority were stolen from one address. He then went into the field to determine the exact environment of the concentration of auto theft and found a multi-deck parking garage as the address from which most cars in the hot spot were stolen.

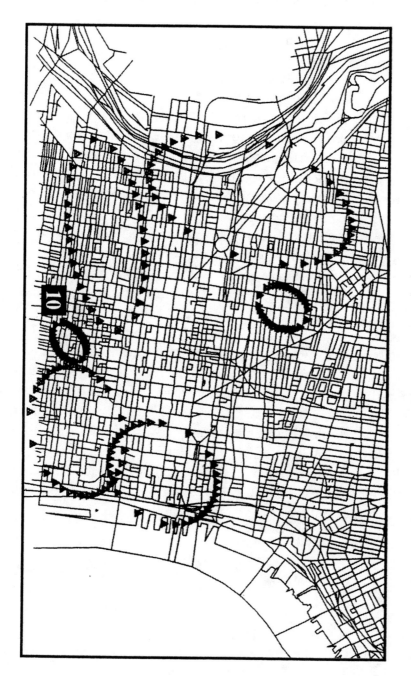

Figure 12: Center City Philadelphia Auto Theft Hot-Spot Analysis

Theoretically, we must question whether we should term this type of concentration of crime a hot spot. Certainly it was a concentration of crime in space in two dimensions. However, the crime occurred in three dimensions on the parking decks. The address-based GIS did not indicate the parking decks on which the auto theft occurred. In fact, it may not have been concentrated in either horizontal or vertical space. In order to determine whether there was a concentration of auto theft in the total space available to auto thieves in the parking garage, Rengert multiplied the street length of the parking garage by the number of parking decks to obtain a conservative estimate of the total space available to auto thieves in the parking garage. This distance was divided in half and compared with the number of cars stolen over this distance in each direction on South Street from the parking garage. As it turned out, there was more auto theft on South Street per foot of street frontage than in the parking garage.

Since the purpose of identifying hot spots is to concentrate patrol, the police would not be allocating patrol in an efficient manner if they were to concentrate patrol on the street in front of the parking garage *or* on the many decks of the parking garage at the expense of the surrounding streets. This is especially true when one considers that the parking garage cannot be patrolled as efficiently (at the same speed) as the surrounding street. This is a case where a false hot spot was identified using a common statistical routine. A high-definition GIS containing a capability for a horizontal and vertical dimension rather than an address point in space would clarify this problem.

An example of the use of high-definition GIS to examine crime in a polygon feature on Temple University's campus is an analysis of the crime patterns in one of its buildings, Gladfelter Hall (see Figure 13). In traditional GIS, all the crimes occurring within the building would be depicted as a point in space associated with the address of the building. This data can be disaggregated in several ways using high-definition GIS.

Figure 13: Gladfelter Hall

Gladfelter Hall

Initially, we disaggregated along the vertical dimension in order to determine whether crimes were clustered on specific floors. Newman (1972) argues that crime will most likely occur on the bottom floors of a high-rise building. In the case of Gladfelter Hall, with the exception of the first floor, we saw that crime was most likely to occur on the upper floors of the building (see Figure 14).

Figure 14: Gladfelter Hall Crime Distribution by Floor

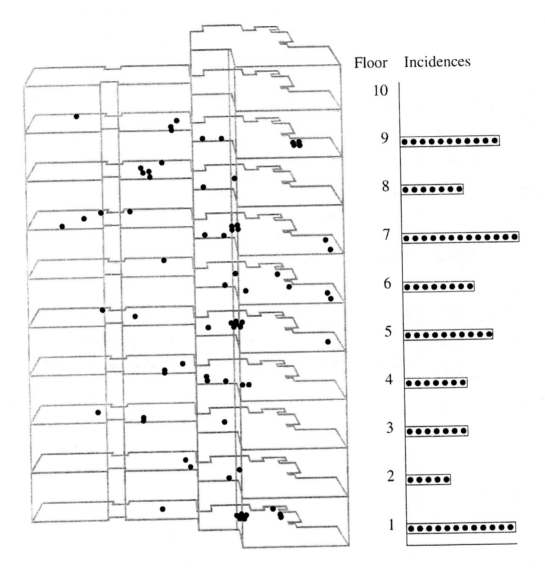

Next, we used the overlay function to analyze the horizontal arrangement of crime within the building. In this case, crime was projected onto the ground floor footprint of the building. This was an aggregation of rare events to determine if there is a feature common to every floor in the building that affected the spatial arrangement of crime. For example, an elevator shaft or staircase may cluster crime about it while more remote parts of the floors may have less crime. Crimes can be color coded to reflect the floor on which they occurred even when projected onto the building footprint.

Figure 15 illustrates the overlay that projected all crimes occurring between 1991 and 1998 in Gladfelter Hall onto the building footprint. There were some clear clusters of crime in this illustration. The largest cluster occurred in the area closest to the bank of four elevators.

Figure 15: Gladfelter Hall Crime on Building Footprint

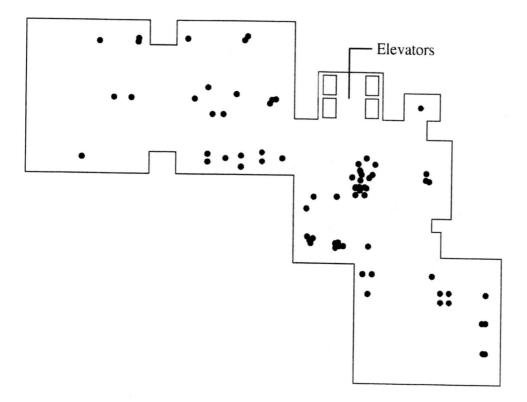

This area contains the secretary and/or receptionist's office on nearly all floors. These offices are commonly referred to as the "fishbowls" since they are surrounded by glass windows which allow one to view the room's contents (see Figure 16). These locational and site characteristics make these rooms especially vulnerable. As a semi-public area, these rooms contain the most pedestrian traffic of any areas in the building except the public entrance.

The Department of Criminal Justice, located on the fifth floor of Gladfelter Hall, altered the site characteristics of this room to decrease its vulnerability. Blinds were installed that may be lowered in the evening when the room is not occupied so that pedestrians cannot observe the room's contents (see Figure 17). This helps secure the computers, telephones, and other office equipment from view of those in the public hallway.

The importance of the elevators as crime generators is also illustrated in the second concentration of crime in offices. Notice in Figure 15 that on exiting the elevators the view to the left is a wall as the hallway turns. The view to the right is an extensive hallway with offices and conference rooms in plain view. Notice that the first offices and conference rooms to the right of the elevators experienced a concentration of crimes. Faculty members in this location should take special care to lock their offices when they are not occupied since pedestrians are more likely to try their doors or to walk into open unoccupied offices in this direction.

Finally, notice that offices at the far end of hallways are the least likely to be the location of crimes. The exception is a design feature of Gladfelter Hall that creates a very vulnerable environment. There is a small cluster of crimes off the hallway to the left of the elevators. In this location, a small hallway makes a horseshoe turn off the main hallway, creating a secluded area that is relatively unused. Since it cannot be seen from the main hallway unless one is standing directly at the turn, it provides a secluded area for criminal activity. Again, faculty in this location should take special care to secure their offices. On some floors, security doors have been installed to limit access to these areas (see Figure 18). Lines interrupting the hallways on the building footprint depict these doors. However, most floors do not have these doors and pedestrians have free access to these locations.

Figure 16: Gladfelter Hall 7th Floor Reception Area

Figure 17: Gladfelter Hall 5th Floor Reception Area

Figure 18: Gladfelter Hall 7th Floor Security Door

The only floor in Gladfelter Hall that has not experienced crime is the tenth floor. This is the top floor in Gladfelter Hall and it has some design features that make it uniquely less vulnerable to criminals (see Figure 19). First, it is a truncated floor, with the hallway and offices to the right of the elevator missing. Therefore, when exiting the elevator, the only possible route is to the left. This hallway is interrupted by a security door. During school hours when this door is unlocked, a receptionist sits facing it. Therefore, this is a very secure area. This floor houses the Center for Public Policy, which is a research arm of the University.

Figure 19: Gladfelter Hall 10th Floor Center for Public Policy

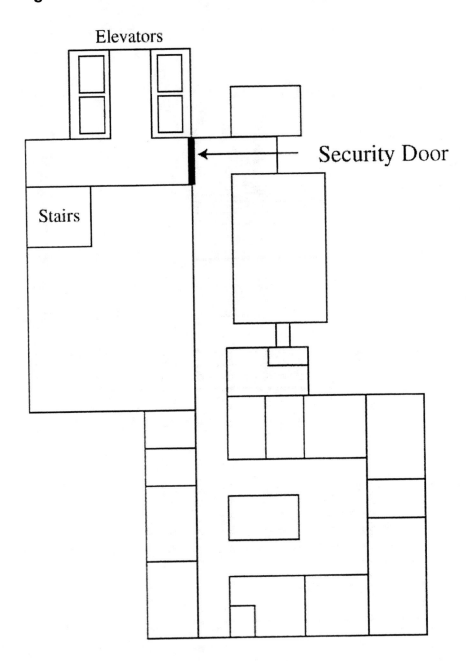

Once a "hot spot" of crime is identified within a building, we must examine the environment that surrounds the hot spot. This is its situation in space. The situation of the hot spot of crime may suggest the best means of control. Situational means of crime control can be identified and evaluated best with high-definition GIS. For example, a traditional GIS may identify a hot spot of crime in the student activity center. A high-definition GIS may determine that the hot spot of crime is in the location of vending machines of the building. Using high-definition GIS, the hot spot of crime can be outlined in a polygon with an associated "attribute table." This "polygon hot spot" delimited by the environment containing the vending machines then provides the base for evaluating situational means of crime control. For example, the vending machines may be secured with hardware to prevent breaking and entering. The security of the surrounding area may be increased using closed-circuit TV or a security guard. In either case, crime within the "polygon hot spot" before the treatment can be compared with crime after the treatment to determine whether the level and/or the nature of the crime has changed. This is possible since the attribute tables record the characteristics as well as the numbers of crimes in the two time periods.

Crime in the "polygon hot spot" also can be compared with crime in the remainder of the building to determine whether the intervention has lowered crime, displaced it to the area beyond the polygon hot spot, or had no effect. Without the delineation of the polygon hot spot, the analyst could not be sure whether the intervention was responsible or whether crime was down for the entire building or campus due to some other factor. In short, high-definition GIS allows the focused evaluation necessary to determine the impact of situational means of crime control.

Chapter V.
Campus Victimization Surveys

A special problem facing urban campuses is that the majority of crimes may not be reported to the police. Whether this unreported crime is randomly scattered about the reported pattern of crime, or whether hot spots of unreported crime may exist that require the attention of the campus community and police, are questions that remain unanswered.

Unreported crime may be characteristic of certain locations. For example, one reason for not reporting crime is that the victim blames himself. He or she may be ashamed because "I should not have been in that place late at night" or "I was not being careful." Also, crime may be "expected" rather than unusual in some locations: "I parked on a neighborhood street and my battery was stolen." A student may reason that it is cheaper to have a battery stolen now and then than to pay to park on a university supervised lot. In all these cases, crime may not be reported to the campus police.

The Temple Victimization Survey

We conducted a "victimization survey" in an attempt to obtain this missing information. The victimization survey was administered to Temple University students, faculty and staff in two waves. The first phase of the survey occurred from April 6th to May 4th of 1998. The sample was selected from the entire population of Temple University students, faculty and staff members who worked or attended school on the main campus. Excluded from the study were those individuals who worked or attended classes at another Temple University campus.

The research team generated a complete list of undergraduate and graduate classes offered during the spring semester of 1998. Lab sections and unusual classes such as "independent study" or "directed research" were excluded from the list. The remaining classes were numbered sequentially, and a table of random numbers was used to select the classes to participate in the research. Eleven survey administrators were trained and sent to administer the survey in a total of 140 classes, resulting in a total of 1,714 usable responses.

The survey was administered to the students in attendance on the day that each class was visited. Survey administrators advised the students that participating in the survey was both voluntary and anonymous. While students who were not in attendance at the time of the survey administration did not participate in the research, administrators experienced only limited refusal to complete the surveys (less than 1%).

Faculty and staff members were selected from a list of all departments in the University. A table of random numbers was used to select departments. Each member of the faculty and staff in that department was administrated a survey. Three hundred surveys were delivered to the mail boxes of the faculty and staff, and 136 completed surveys were returned. The first wave of the survey resulted in a total of 1,950 responses.

The 1998 victimization survey consisted of four sections. The first section elicited background information on age, race, sex and rank in college. It also solicited general background information on campus activities in which the respondent participates, the respondent's mode of transportation to campus, and the amount of time that the respondent spends on campus. The second section was designed to measure respondents' perceptions of safety on campus in the daytime and nighttime. This section included two maps of the greater university. One of the maps represented the campus during the nighttime, while the other represented the campus during the daytime. Both were divided into 20 sections. Each of the maps asked the respondent to identify the section perceived to be the most safe and rate it a 10. The respondent was then asked to identify the section perceived to be the least safe and rate it a 0. The remaining sections were rated between 0 and 10, depending on whether the respondent perceived it to be more like the safest or least safe area.

The third section contained questions concerning any crime the respondent may have experienced on or around campus. This section solicited information on five categories of victimization: theft, vandalism, assault, sex crimes, and other. The survey asked the respondent for specific details as to time, date and location of the victimization. The fourth section was designed to measure the amount of time and space the respondent used on campus on an average day. This section provided information about the use of the campus temporally and geographically so that research could control for time and space at risk.

The second wave of the victimization survey was administered between March 22, 1999 and April 9, 1999. The research team used the same method to select the sample of 250 classes. The faculty and staff were surveyed in the same manner as the first wave of the victimization survey. The second survey resulted in 1,866 completed usable surveys. All data obtained from the 1998 and 1999 victimization surveys were coded, checked and entered into a database that is used for this analysis.

Summary Survey Statistics

Temple University is a comprehensive public research university with approximately 28,000 students. Founded in 1884, Temple is one of Pennsylvania's three public research universities, along with the University of Pittsburgh and the Pennsylvania State University. The main campus is located in Philadelphia, Pennsylvania, with five regional campuses around the state and world. Temple University is the 35th largest university in the United States.

Over 73% of Temple University's students are residents of Pennsylvania. Most are from the city of Philadelphia and commute to campus. The ethnicity of Temple students is given in Table 2. Just under 56% of these students are women and 44.2% are men. There are 1,567 full-time faculty members.

Table 2: The Ethnicity of Temple Students

Ethnicity	Enrollment	Percent
White	15,957	58.8
Black	5,638	20.8
Asian	2,997	11.0
Hispanic	927	3.4
Other	1,638	6.0
International Students 1,106		

The respondents to both the 1998 and 1999 surveys resemble closely the race, gender and age of the university's population. Males constituted just under 43% (42.7) of the population surveyed in 1998, while females made up the remaining 57.2% of survey respondents. Similarly, 43.5% of the 1999 survey respondents were male, with females accounting for 56.5%. Fewer than one-quarter of the students surveyed lived on campus (20.5% in 1998; 22.5% in 1999). The large majority of respondents lived off campus. Over 65% (67.4% in 1998; 66.6% in 1999) of those living off campus lived within Philadelphia county. Thirty-two percent (1998) and 33.4% (1999) commuted from outside the city limits.

Table 3 lists the ethnicity of the survey respondents. Note that it resembles closely the ethnicity of the total student population listed in Table 1. It was decided to use classroom interviews rather than telephone or mail interviews in order to improve on the "hit rate" of previous studies. For example, Fisher, Sloan and Wilkins (1995) had a response rate of 24.7% from surveys mailed to students. In contrast, Rand and Levine (1989) obtained a response rate of 80% by administering questionnaires directly to UCLA students rather than relying on mailed surveys. By surveying students in classroom settings, we also had very few students (less than 1%) who refused to fill out the survey.

Table 3: Ethnicity of Survey Respondents

	1998 Respondents		1999 Respondents	
	Total	**Percent**	**Total**	**Percent**
White	1,089	55.8	1,069	57.3
Black	493	25.3	385	20.6
Hispanic	66	3.4	59	3.2
Asian	212	10.8	233	12.5
Other	59	3.0	90	4.8
Total	1,929		1,836	

Just over one-quarter (26.8%) of the respondents to the 1998 survey reported at least one victimization experience while on the university campus. (This statistic contrasts with nearly 40% of the respondents who reported being a victim of crime in a national random sample of 10,000 undergraduates [Bausell et al., 1991]). While 19.3% reported being victimized once, 4.8% reported two victimization experiences, and 2.7% of the respondents reported three or more victimization experiences. Male respondents reported slightly higher victimization rates (27.8%) than females (26.1%). White respondents reported the highest victimization rates (29.8%) among university students and employees, with Hispanic respondents reporting a similar rate (28.8%). While Asians reported fewer victimization experiences (23.9%), African Americans reported the lowest victimization rates (21.3%). Of those victimized, 62.1% were white, 20.1% were black, 8.6% were Asian and 3.6% were Hispanic.

As expected, the number of years spent on campus was correlated with the amount of victimization ever experienced. Faculty and staff reported the highest victimization rate (66.2%) among survey respondents. Thirty-two percent of graduate students and 28.2% of seniors stated that they had been victimized. Freshman reported the lowest victimization rates (17.5%), with sophomores and juniors reporting slightly higher rates (21.9% and 21.8%, respectively). Thirty percent of the respondents who lived on campus reported victimization, while fewer (25.9%) of those who commuted to campus reported victimization.

Twenty-two percent reported being victims of theft, 1.1% reported experiencing auto theft, and 6.8% fell victim to vandalism. Fewer than 7% of the respondents reported suffering violent crimes, with 6.5% reporting incidents of assault and 0.1% reporting sexual assaults. Thefts constituted 58.6% of all victimizations, auto theft made up 3% and vandalism accounted for 18%. Assault and sexual assault accounted for the remaining 17.1% and 2.6%, respectively.

Less than half of all victimization (38.8%) recorded in the survey was reported to the university police department. Auto theft was the most reported incident (77.3%), followed by theft (42.8%) and vandalism (31.8%). These high reporting rates can be explained by the need for a police report in order to file an insurance claim for stolen or damaged property (especially an automobile). Victims were less likely to report assaults (27.8%) and sexual assaults (21.1%). Of those who did not report incidents to the police, 13.6% cited insignificant loss or damage as the reason for their decision. Thirty-three percent of respondents chose not to involve the police because they felt that the police could not do anything about the incident. A small number of respondents (2.3%) reported that they were too afraid to call the police, and 12.5% claimed that reporting their victimization to the police takes too much time.

Follow-up Survey

In the spring of 1999 another survey was drawn. This survey repeated the questions asked in the prior year. The intent of this data collection was to obtain post-intervention information about police and community responses to the "hot spots" identified in the previous year. Therefore, while the 1998 survey asked respondents to report all victimization by year of occurrence, the follow-up survey asked respondents for information about victimization occurring only during the past year.

Twelve and one-half percent of the respondents to the 1999 survey reported victimization in the past year. Just under 12% reported one victimization, 0.8% reported two victimizations and 0.1% reported three or more victimization experiences. Males and females had similar victimization experiences (12.9% for males and 12.3% for females). However, of those victimized, 44.9% were male and 55.1% were female.

Asian-American respondents reported the highest victimization rates (14.7%) in this survey, followed by Hispanics (13.6%), whites (13.2%) and blacks (10.1%). White respondents made up the majority of those victimized (60.3%). Blacks accounted for 16.7% and Asians for 13.7% of reported victimization incidents. Fewer than 4% (3.4%) of the victimized respondents were Hispanic.

Undergraduate students reported similar victimization experiences, with juniors reporting the lowest rates (10.2%) and sophomores reporting the highest (14.8%). Among faculty and staff, 12.8% reported being victimized, while 12.3% of graduate students experienced victimization. Those respondents who lived on campus reported higher victimization rates (14.1%) than those who commuted to the university (12.1%).

Most victimizations involved property crime, with 8.9% of respondents reporting theft, 0.2% reporting auto theft and 2.6% reporting vandalism. Assaults affected 1.3% of respondents, while 0.4% of respondents fell victim to sexual assault. Theft (66.4%), auto theft (1.6%) and vandalism (19.2%) accounted for almost 90% of all victimization. Assault (10.0%) and sexual assault (2.8%) comprised the remaining victimization.

Information from the initial victimization survey was plotted using high-definition GIS, and hot spots of crime were identified. The environmental situation of each hot spot was examined and a polygon drawn around the environmental situation associated with each cluster of crimes (see Figure 20). The hot spots identified from the victimization data were compared with those reported to the police to determine if there are locations where students are less likely to report crime (perhaps because it is expected) than others (where they are shocked to be victimized). The differences in the spatial patterns of crime were identified, and the environments and situations associated with each pattern examined to explain the differences and to design remedial action. For example, Temple University Police may devise a campaign targeted at situations of unreported crime in order to improve the comprehensiveness of reported crime. Temple police administrators feel strongly that campus crime should not be concealed from the campus community or the public. In fact, campus crime is regularly reported by address and type of crime in the student newspaper.

When we compared reported crime with victimization survey data, an important difference was obvious between the two police kiosks on the way from the main campus to the commuter train station. The police data had no reports of assaults or violent crime other than street robbery on this route. However, the first victimization survey illustrated an important concentration of assaults on this route. The question arises as to why these crimes were not reported to the police.

There are two possible explanations for why the incidents on the route to the train station were not reported to the police. The first is that they were relatively minor, such as neighborhood kids throwing dirt at students. Students may expect some of this behavior as they walk through an urban neighborhood of public-assisted housing. The second reason is that the victim might miss a train or class if time was taken to report an incident. The police now know that more is happening along this route than was reflected in their records.

Preventive Measures

Temple University Police were shown the "victimization hot spots" as well as the "reported crime hot spots." Preventive actions were identified and implemented in consultation between the police, students and academic professionals. The second victimization survey was conducted to determine if victimization patterns had changed from the previous years (see Figure 21). Special attention was paid to the "victimization hot spots" identified in the previous year that had been provided with treatment. In this manner, we determined whether the intervention strategies had succeeded. The high-definition GIS and the victimization hot spots of 1998 provided us with leads of what should be done (improving lighting, altering land-scaping, heightening student awareness of dangerous situations, encouraging more complete reporting of crime, controlling access, preventive patrol, etc.). The second victimization survey determined whether crime had changed after treatment in the polygons defined by the victimization hot spots. Police data determined whether crime had changed after treatment in reported crime hot spots.

Figure 20: Temple University Victimization
Assaults 1997-98 Academic Year

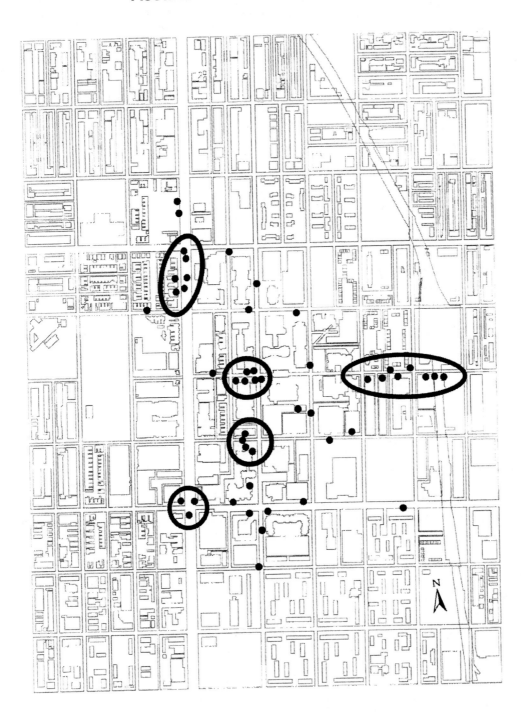

The most dramatic change occurred in the amount and distribution of assaults on campus. Figure 20 illustrates that there were five concentrations in the earlier survey. The most troubling was a concentration of six assaults near the center of campus. This location is dominated by a sculpture of an owl, the mascot of Temple University (see Figure 22). A second concentration was outside the student activity center, another was near a public transportation station, and the final one was outside the student dormitory complex. Several remedial actions were taken to address these problem areas. First, many of the assaults occurred during "Spring Fling," a student celebration each spring. In the past, big name bands were contracted and the event was advertised widely in the Philadelphia region. This attracted many young people who wanted to participate in the free concert and drink alcohol. Spring Fling 1999 was scaled down considerably. Local bands were hired, and the event was not advertised in the Philadelphia region. Crowds were sparser and more controllable. These changes may account for the absence of assaults around the Owl Sculpture in the following year.

The cluster of assaults outside the student dormitories also created concern. Two measures were taken to address this situation. First, a local drinking establishment was closed on Broad Street. Temple had previously opened a drinking establishment on campus that could be more closely controlled. Secondly, the Temple police changed patrol practices to address this problem area. Bike patrol was added to this location, a daily patrol from 7 a.m. to 2 a.m.

Attention was paid to the cluster of assaults occurring between the campus and the commuter train station. Temple University police increased escort services along paths to public transportation stations and parking facilities. In the 1997-98 academic year, student and police pedestrian efforts provided approximately 33,000 escorts. Escort services were increased the following year with the addition of two vans to the shuttle route. The police escort service was advertised in fliers and campus safety brochures. This resulted in over 64,000 escorts throughout the 1998-99 academic year, eliminating some of the nighttime foot traffic to the train and subway stations.

Finally, new construction on campus resulted in the closing of 13th Street to all through traffic. It also restricted public street parking. While students could still walk through the area, access was limited and no cars could pass through. The street was fenced at 13th Street from Montgomery Avenue to Norris Street.

Figure 21: Temple University Victimization Assaults 1998-99 Academic Year

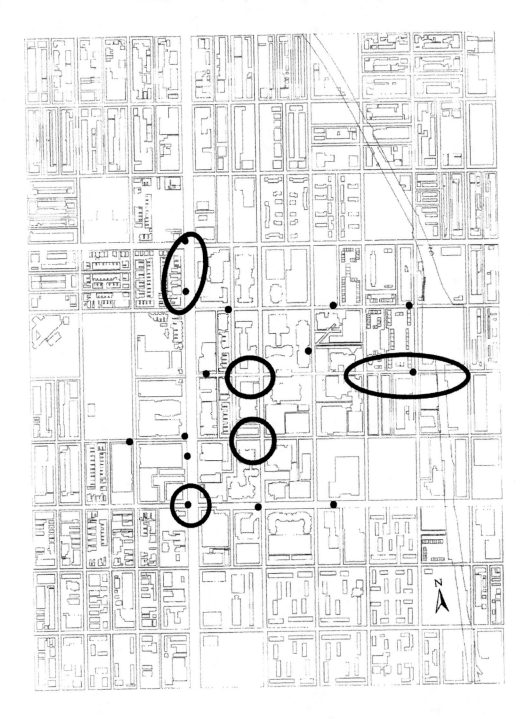

Figure 22: Temple Owl

The follow-up survey in 1999 illustrates dramatic change. Assaults were dramatically fewer and there were no spatial clusters of this crime (see Figure 21). Most important, the center of campus had no assaults identified in the follow-up survey. In fact, the Temple University Police only had 30 violent crimes reported in total (including assault, rape, robbery and murder) during this period, down from 114 in 1995. This is a very commendable record of progress.

Fear of Crime on Campus

The victimization surveys also contained a section designed to gauge perceptions of dangerous areas in and around Temple University's main campus. This area was divided into 20 sections (the area in the center of campus was subdivided into six zones). The students, faculty and staff were presented with this map and asked to identify the most dangerous location and assign it a 0. Then they were asked to identify the safest area and assign it a 10. Other areas were then scaled by whether they were most like the safest or most dangerous zone. This exercise was completed twice, once for the daytime and once for nighttime perceptions of safety.

The results of this exercise were analyzed, giving each zone an average score for perceived daytime safety (see Figure 23) and perceived nighttime safety (see Figure 24). These figures were then compared with actual crime occurring outside buildings within each zone. The crime occurring in the subdivided middle area was summed to correct for the fact that each was one-sixth the size of the other areas. Finally, contour lines, which generalize the daytime and nighttime data, were constructed for both the perceived safety map and the map of actual violent crime (see Figures 23, 24, and 25).

As these three figures illustrate, the users of Temple University's campus and surrounding neighborhoods did not accurately match the levels of actual crime with their perceptions of safety. The area they felt was the safest (around the student activity center) actually experienced a great deal of crime. The areas they felt were the most dangerous (the surrounding community) actually exhibited relatively little crime. This may be due to the fact that students, faculty and staff avoided areas in which they did not feel comfortable. Because of such avoidance, the "opportunity for crime" victimization may be lower in the neighborhoods surrounding Temple University's main campus than in the center of the campus.

Comparing Temple and Penn

Temple University is largely a commuter campus. The university's main campus in North Philadelphia houses just 15% of its student population on campus. Unlike many residential campuses, Temple's surrounding community offers little opportunity for shopping or entertainment. Students rarely travel into the surrounding community. Rather, students tend to remain on campus or travel outside of North Philadelphia to other parts of the city to socialize. As a result, Temple has a relatively low crime rate compared to other urban institutions of higher education.

Figure 23: Perceived Daytime Safety

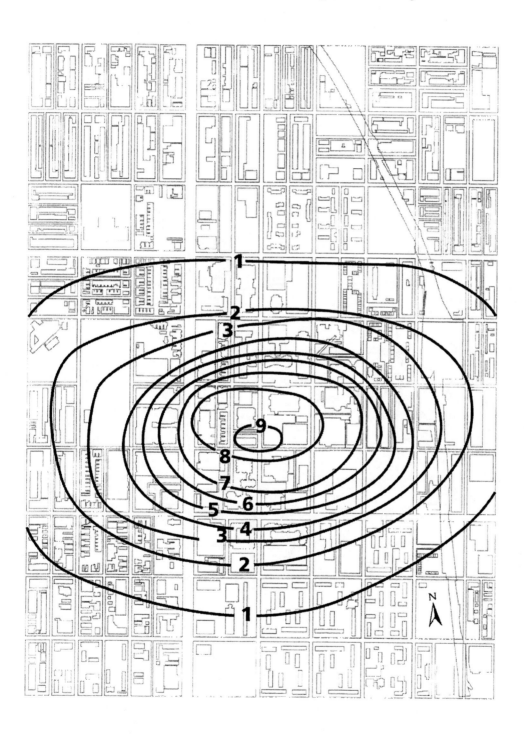

Figure 24: Perceived Nighttime Safety

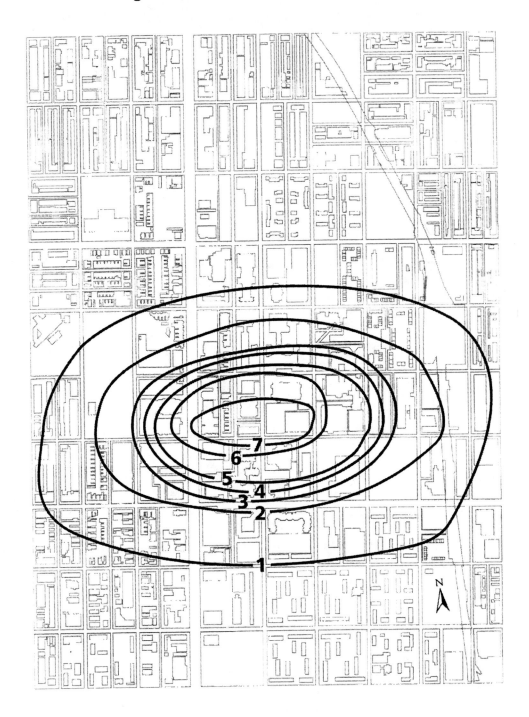

Figure 25: Actual Reported Violent Crime

Contrary to local opinion, Temple University has a lower crime rate than the University of Pennsylvania, which is also located in inner-city Philadelphia. The University of Pennsylvania is a residential campus set in West Philadelphia. A comparison of the 1998 crime statistics published by each of the universities demonstrates the differences in crime on the campuses. The universities serve similar numbers of students. The University of Pennsylvania has approximately 22,000 students, and Temple University has about 21,000 on its main campus. Residents of the surrounding communities have access to both institutions.

As illustrated in Table 4, the two universities both suffered one homicide in 1998. The University of Pennsylvania experienced one rape, while Temple University had no reported rapes. The University of Pennsylvania reported 39 robberies and 15 aggravated assaults, while Temple University had only 3 robberies. Property crime presents similar differences. The University of Pennsylvania received reports of 73 burglaries, 879 thefts and 22 auto thefts. Temple University received reports of 14 burglaries, 165 thefts and 2 auto thefts. Temple University also reported fewer Part Two offenses (see Table 4).

While some of these differences in crime numbers between the two universities result from the varying percentage of students living on campus, several other reasons may be responsible for the lower crime numbers at Temple University. Temple University students do not perceive the communities surrounding Temple University's main campus as safe (see Figures 23 and 24). Therefore, they are less likely to use this area and are very aware of their surroundings when they do. Students at the University of Pennsylvania, on the other hand, do not perceive the communities surrounding their campus as dangerous relative to North Philadelphia. Therefore, they are more likely to live and socialize in and around their campus.

Table 4: Crime on Two Campuses

Classification of Offenses	Temple University	University of Pennsylvania
Part I		
Homicide	1	1
Rape	0	1
Robbery	3	39
Aggravated Assault	0	15
Burglary	14	73
Theft	165	879
Auto Theft	2	22
Part II		
Simple Assault	10	32
Forgery	2	0
Fraud	5	20
Rec. Stolen Property	0	1
Vandalism	44	156

CHAPTER VI.
SUMMARY AND CONCLUSIONS

A common conception is that college campuses are idyllic havens to which young people go to be transformed into adults. In reality, this may not be far from the truth. Campuses generally have far less crime than the communities in which they are located. Yet any crime is serious on a university campus. The economic viability of the university hinges on the public's perception of the relative safety of the campus. Therefore, campus crime is a serious problem. The communications media have exploited the difference between people's perceptions of campuses and the reality of campus crime by sensationalizing high profile incidents of crime on American campuses (Kalette, 1990). Books have been written to prepare prospective students and their parents to cope with their new home away from home (Bromley and Territo, 1990; Smith and Smith, 1990). Finally, politicians were influenced by public pressure and enacted bills to inform prospective students of crime on campuses (Student Right-To-Know and Campus Security Act of 1990).

University administrators realize that the perception of crime on their campuses seriously affects the rate of future applications. They began to place priority on campus police and security in an attempt to reduce crime and victimization. Most large universities have police departments that mirror municipal police departments in administration and training. However, there are important differences. One reason colleges and universities have developed their own police departments rather than rely on the police from the surrounding community is so that they can exercise greater control over the activities of the campus police. For example, they can assign campus police to crowd control at a sporting event, for which they may not feel entitled to demand scarce police resources needed in and paid for by the taxpayers of the surrounding community. They may require campus police to randomly patrol within buildings that police from the surrounding community are not required to patrol. Finally, they may focus on preventing crime rather than apprehending criminals, because once a crime is committed on a university campus the damage has been done. In short, campus administrators wish campus police to focus on special problems of the campus community. The majority of these problems require high-definition GIS to identify and record.

Several sections of this book describe a high-definition GIS system that incorporates the three dimensions of the built environment. This system allows a micro-level identification and location of crime necessary for modern analysis of community policing and situational crime control. With this tool in hand, we can map information from a victimization survey of unreported crime, as well as crime reported to the police, to determine the exact situation and environment in which the crime took place. High-definition GIS allows a more refined reporting of crime to the campus community and suggests joint actions that the community and police can undertake to regain control of a criminogenic situation. Thus, high-definition GIS highlights the remedial actions to be taken and provides the infrastructure for evaluating the success of the remedial actions.

APPENDIX 1.
GEOGRAPHIC TOOLS FOR POLICING SMALL AREAS

In Chapter II, we developed the theme that college campuses are self-contained entities that are not affected to a great degree by the criminogenic characteristics of neighborhoods that surround them. Campus environments are very different from their surroundings. When one steps onto a college campus, the differences are generally apparent. Buildings change from residential to multistory office and classroom structures. Landscaping changes from residential or commercial to institutional. Sometimes, one passes under a gate or archway symbolizing the change in the character of the environment.

The character of police functions also changes when one sets foot on a college campus. We have discussed the development of law enforcement on campuses and the importance of community policing techniques for campus security. Many municipal and campus security administrators have adopted community policing techniques. However, there are important differences between campus and municipal policing. For example, campus and municipal police departments are responsible for patrolling different environments. Campus police, like public housing police, patrol a much smaller area than municipal police. Further, campus and housing police may be required to patrol within buildings — a task for which municipal police are not directly responsible. Therefore, different modes of record keeping and analysis may be necessary. While street addresses may suffice as units of reference for municipal police record-keeping and analysis, campus police may wish to record incidents by the floor of a building or even by office or room on a floor of a building. In short, campus police require a more refined method of storing spatial and temporal information. This requires a modified type of Geographic Information System.

In the following discussion, we illustrate how a high-definition GIS differs from a traditional version. Much of this material is technical. We begin with a description of traditional GIS.

Traditional Geographic Information Systems

The typical GIS employed by municipal police is a city or countywide system that uses a large area/small scale format suitable to the large size of the coverage area. Addressable single lines depict streets, and the built environment is completely absent (see Figure 26). In this conventional application, the lack of detail is an acceptable trade-off for the ability to use GIS software to plot crime locations and look for patterns and "hot spots" over relatively large areas.

Although county- and municipal-level GIS enables effective small-scale analysis of relatively large areas, storing information at the street address becomes problematic when more than one incident occurs at a single address. Address-based record-keeping does not account for the varying opportunities for crime at a given address. This method fails to account for building size in either the horizontal or vertical dimensions when recording incidents. For example, some buildings may be hundreds of feet in length and width while others are small. Yet, each is associated with a single address. Parking may be limited to a surface lot or dispersed in a multi-decked garage. Address-based record-keeping assigns all the crime that occurs in a building to a single point in space, thus ignoring the location of incidents within and around a building.

Conventional GIS also presents problems with "hot spot" analysis. Identifying "hot spots" of crime by the number of occurrences that cluster in horizontal space, rather than the number of occurrences per total area or opportunities for crime, can cause misleading interpretations or identifications of "hot spots" of crime. Hot-spot analysis that is based only on the building address will tend to identify large multi-story buildings as hot spots of crime, since they contain more people and/or opportunities for crime. For example, Wilkins (1996) identified hospitals as hot spots of crime on the University of Alabama at Birmingham's campus, as measured by the number of incidents per building on campus. Clearly, building size must be considered before we can identify a true hot spot of crime. What is required is a refined geographic information system: a high-definition GIS.

A High-Definition Geographic Information System

A high-definition GIS highlights the specific locations of crimes within and around buildings at an address. Ideally, such a system may locate a hot spot of crime on the eighth floor of a college dormitory rather than in "Old East Hall" for exam-

Figure 26: Traditional GIS, Center City Philadelphia

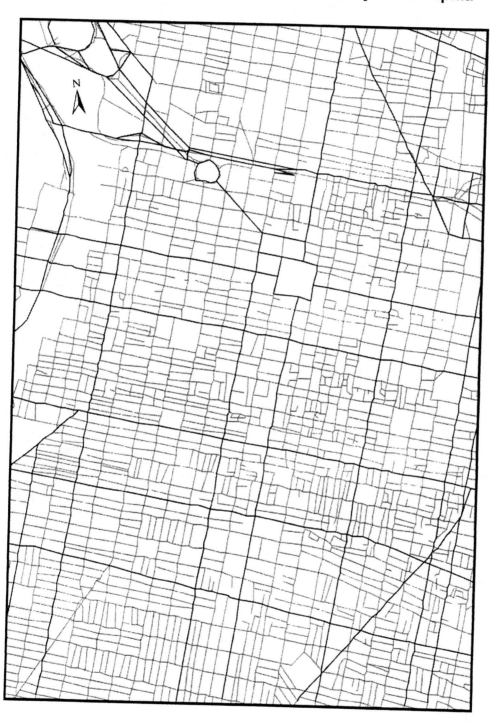

ple. The concentration of crime or vandalism on the eighth floor of Old East Hall will tell a campus police officer and the campus community much more of what needs to be known than a simple building address. Furthermore, the accurate records required by federal and state laws will be facilitated by a high-definition GIS that tells the analyst which floor the incident occurred on.

The "Student Right-To-Know and Campus Security Act" (1990) requires all post-secondary institutions receiving federal financial aid to publish statistics on the number of serious violent crimes reported to campus police, as well as drug, alcohol, and weapons violations detected on campus. Therefore, exactly where an offense occurs is important to campus administrators who want to portray their campuses as safe places. If most crime occurs on the edge of the campus in the surrounding community (Brantingham et al., 1995), the side of the street on which the incident occurred — or whether it occurred on the campus sidewalk versus the public street — is important information.

High-definition GIS also provides the community with accurate statistics and analysis that are much less likely to be misinterpreted. The more refined record-keeping and analysis possible with a high-definition geographic information system enhances the information available to the public.

In the following case study, we will focus attention on a campus ranked as one of the ten most dangerous in the nation by the APBnews.com report (1999) — Temple University in Philadelphia, Pennsylvania. Temple University is an urban campus in inner city Philadelphia that many expect to be associated with a high violent crime rate. However, as observed in Table 1, Temple University was in the middle (267 of 470 colleges) of schools ranked by violent crime per 1,000 students. Temple University police use GIS to combat crime. The GIS techniques developed for Temple University also apply to any small, contained environment such as a public housing project, a shopping mall, or a special service district in the center of a city. They also apply to other college campuses.

The Development of a High-Definition GIS

Most urban campuses are relatively small compact spaces. Using the Temple University main campus located in north Philadelphia as an example, the *campus proper* (defined by the location of university classrooms, labs, dormitories, athletic facilities, administrative offices, and support buildings) is a mere 36 square blocks covering 95 acres of land in North Philadelphia (see Figure 27). The Temple Uni-

Figure 27: Temple University's Effective Campus

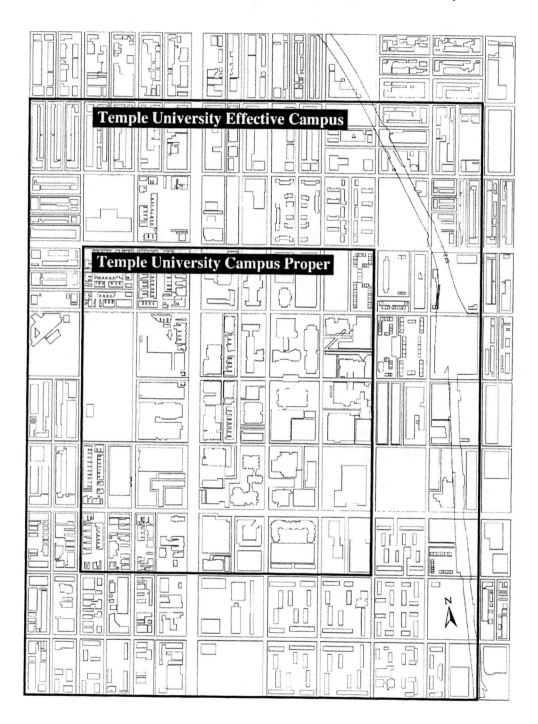

versity police patrol the *effective campus*, which is defined as the campus proper plus a two block perimeter consisting of the surrounding neighborhoods (see Figure 27). The effective campus totals 144 square blocks, and represents less than 1% of the entire city (see Figure 28).

From Figure 28, it should be apparent why a GIS appropriate for the city as a whole would not be appropriate for a relatively small area such as Temple University, or a public housing project, or a center city district.

The cartographic solution to the problem of depicting a small area in detail is to use a small-area/large-scale format base map that increases the level of detail represented on the base map. Geographic detail included in a high-definition campus security GIS may include roadways portrayed by their two curb lines, sidewalks, common grounds, and building interiors that include multiple floors. This level of detail makes possible the discrete location of an incident: in the street, on which side of the street, on the sidewalk, in a building, on which floor or office in the building, or on the grounds surrounding a building. The construction of such a geographic information system is rather technical. Since it is a new procedure, we will discuss these technical aspects in a step-by-step manner using Temple University as an example.

A. Initial Digitizing

The campus proper (as defined in the previous section) originates as an AutoCad drawing of the campus provided by the facilities management department of the university (Figure 29 is an example from Temple University). These drawings are typically very detailed, depicting lines in parking lots, electrical wiring and water pipes in buildings, and other detail used by architects for construction plans. This unneeded detail must be eliminated since a GIS program will name and provide a storage location for each (for example each line in a parking lot). The editing also includes making sure all polygons are closed and that the only geometry left on the drawing serves the purposes of providing discrete locations (see Figure 27). The editing of the AutoCad drawing is a one-time operation that needs to be repeated only in the event of physical changes to the campus.

At this stage we have acquired a two-dimensional model of the effective campus. It is a simple drawing of the effective campus with no means of assigning characteristics or qualities (termed attributes) to the drawings. This requires that the CAD drawings be imported into a GIS environment. This process is termed building the topology.

Figure 28: Temple University in Philadelphia County

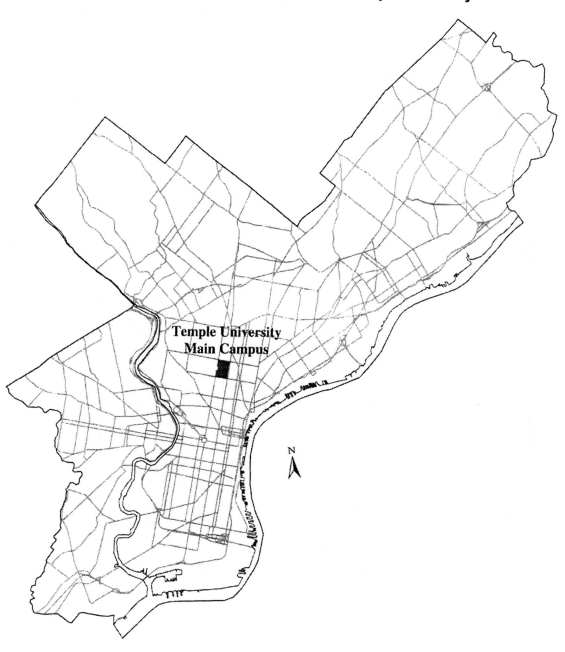

Temple University
Main Campus

Figure 29: Temple University AutoCad Drawing

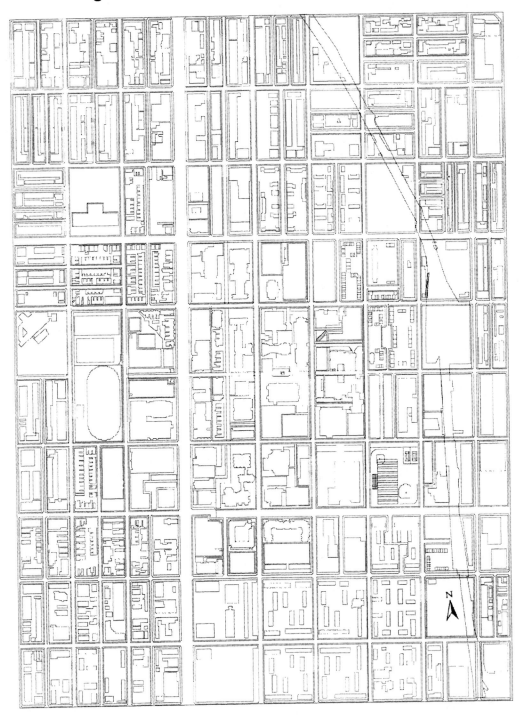

B. Building Topology

Once the digitizing is complete, the Autocad drawing is imported into ARC/INFO (or similar GIS). ARC/INFO creates the GIS coverage by building the "Attribute Tables" for each polygon, point, or line in the drawing. The attribute tables are relational databases within which each polygon, point, or line identified on the two-dimensional model is given a unique ID number. The ID number connects each element of the drawing with an attribute table. Additional fields can be added to the attribute tables so that building ID codes, building height and size can be added to the building polygon attribute tables. The type of offense, time of offense, date of offense, victim name, responding officer name, presence of weapon, and other information can be added to point attribute tables that depict crime locations. Finally, street and sidewalk characteristics (one way, width, etc.) can be added to the line attribute tables. Like the initial digitizing, this is a one-time operation that needs to be repeated only in the event of physical changes to the campus or additions to the attribute tables.

C. Display and Analysis

Following the topology building and the modifications to the attribute tables, the GIS may be imported into ARCVIEW or a similar GIS that is more user-friendly than ARC/INFO. It is from within ARCVIEW that maps are produced as a result of queries to the relational databases contained within the attribute tables. ARCVIEW contains commands to build the query using any combination of attributes contained within the attribute tables. For example, any polygon that contains an attribute that has been requested by a query will be highlighted. Common queries include the location of any police activity in the last 24 hours, the burglaries in the past week, or the events in which a weapon was displayed during a given month. Once the locations of the activities are established, the reader may query any one, and use the associated point attribute table to obtain information on other attributes of the offense. If the analyst is interested in the spatial or temporal pattern of crime, she or he can print a map, the extent of which can be adjusted to show activity within the desired area (campus, building complex, or building).

A problem facing the analyst is that all the information to this point is displayed in two dimensions. The analyst has no way to know by looking at the map which floor or which office or laboratory on a floor the offense occurred. Since most campuses are filled with multi-storied buildings, this information is critical to understanding the true pattern and nature of criminal offenses. Therefore, a GIS system for a college campus or similar area must contain a vertical dimension.

D. Adding the Vertical Component to GIS

The above sections describe the construction of a GIS of the effective campus at the ground level. At first glance, adding a vertical dimension to a mapping routine may seem a trivial task. After all, the vertical dimensions of mountain ranges have been mapped for centuries, and crime rates have been portrayed as peaks and valleys over an urban landscape (Brantingham and Brantingham, 1984; LeBeau, 1995) (see Figure 30). The physical sciences have used 2.5-D and 3-D mapping to depict mineral deposits, water tables, and porosity zones (Raper and Kelk, 1991). A continuous vertical variable, however, is not useful in a GIS of the built environment; after all, no one commits a crime on the ceiling. It is necessary to depict the floors of a building and floor space per floor no matter what the exact height of the building in feet. In other words, the vertical dimension of crime must be mapped in discrete layers (floors of buildings) rather than as a continuous variable (feet of elevation).

The coverage provided by a GIS of the ground level serves as a starting point. Separate coverages are required to display criminal activity in either basements or on floors above the ground. Facilities Management provides the CAD drawings of each floor of all campus buildings, including the stairways and elevators leading to each floor. We first create a coverage containing all of the first floors on campus using the techniques described above (clean the CAD drawings, create a GIS, transport the GIS to ARCVIEW). The same procedure would apply to all second floors in each building on campus, all third floors, fourth floors, etc., until all floors are contained in a coverage.

Campus police now can locate crime on any level of any building. When the system is queried, buildings in which police activity resulted in a record would be highlighted. Further examination of the individual building would reveal the floor on which an activity took place. For example, if an incident occurred on the eighth floor, an analyst would know to use the eighth floor coverage to locate the exact location of the crime on that floor. Then, by clicking on the exact location of the crime, the point attribute table would provide the attributes or distinguishing characteristics of the crime.

These coverages were constructed for the campus proper. The base map, containing the street-level built environment, serves as a reference for each additional

Figure 30: Vertical Mapping

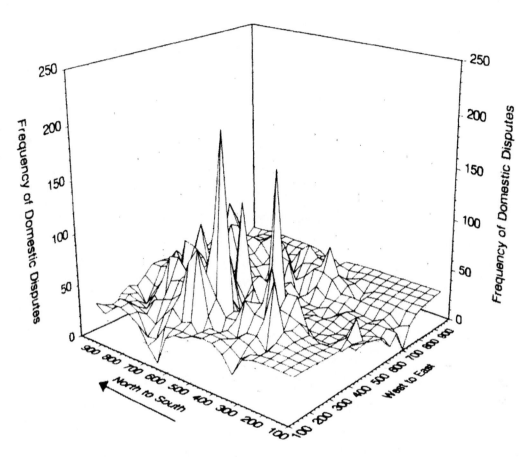

Source: LeBeau, J.L. (1993). "Temporal Ecology of Calls for Police Service"
Workshop on Crime Analysis through Computer Mapping Proceedings: 1993.
Eds. C.R. Block and M. Dabdoub. Chicago: Illinois Criminal Information Authority. (p. 159).

coverage. The final product provides the campus police with a high-definition GIS, which not only allows them to locate crimes precisely for reporting purposes, but also enables them to conduct analysis not possible with traditional GIS. For example, the campus police may wish to know the distribution of crimes occurring in basements of all buildings on campus. A query of the basement coverage(s) of the campus can identify this pattern of crime. On the other hand, the police analyst may combine all the coverages for a specific building in order to determine all the crime that occurred within the specified building.

High-definition GIS allows crime analysts to address questions that are not possible to answer with traditional GIS. For example, is there a cluster or hot spot of crime in the vertical dimension within a campus building? What is the spatial pattern of crime in the various levels of a football stadium? Is it related to student seating, seating of the visiting team's followers, or general admission seating? In Chapter III, we illustrated how high-definition GIS can answer these and other questions concerning situational crime control and community policing.

APPENDIX 2.
THREE-DIMENSIONAL HOT-SPOT ANALYSIS

In Chapter IV, we noted that crime can also be analyzed in three dimensions, considering simultaneously its vertical and horizontal components. This is accomplished by considering the building as a cube within which crime locations are plotted. There are at least two approaches to the analysis of the degree to which crimes are clustered within this cube. The first is to construct the smallest sphere possible that contains the entire building. The volume contained within this sphere is given by the formula 4/3 pi r³ (see Figure 32).

Next, construct the smallest sphere possible that contains all the locations of crimes within the building. The volume of this sphere is then compared with the volume of the sphere containing the entire building to determine the degree of clustering of crimes within the building (see Figure 33). Finally, to determine the degree of clustering within the pattern of crime, gradually reduce the size of the sphere containing all the crimes until it contains a third (or other fraction of your choice). If there is no significant clustering of crime in the three dimensions, this sphere should be one-third the volume of the sphere containing all the crimes (see Figure 34). The degree to which this sphere is less than one-third of the volume of the sphere containing all the crimes is the degree of clustering of crimes within the general pattern of crime. Although this technique identifies the general clustering of crime within the building, it does not identify specific hot spots of crime within the building.

In order to identify and locate the hot spots of crime within the building, a slight modification of this method is required. In this case, the sphere containing all the crimes in the building is reduced gradually from the top and sides maintaining the bottom position since crimes are generally clustered in the bottom floors of a building (Newman, 1972). As the sphere is gradually reduced in size, note the size of the sphere each time a crime is no longer within the sphere. The number of crimes remaining in the sphere being reduced in size can be graphed sequentially with the volume of the sphere (see Figure 31). This graph highlights the location of clusters of crime within the building. In a simple case, if the graph is convex, crimes are clustered near the top and outside edge of the building. If the graph is concave, crimes are clustered near the center and the bottom of the building. Note the distance between the points on these graphs. The location of crime clusters within the building can be identified by those areas on the graph where several crimes exit the sphere without recognizable reduction in the volume of the sphere. Again, these are the points that are located closest together on the graph; the analyst may identify hot spots of crime within the building by the location of points on the graphs that are significantly closer together than others.

A criticism of the spherical method of analysis of crime in three dimensions is that much of the area contained in the sphere is not contained in the building. This is not critical when one is comparing the relative sizes of the spheres. However, a closer approximation to the size of the building can be obtained by using a cube rather than a sphere.

The second method developed by Henderson (1999) is to construct a cube containing a set of small cubes that can be reduced to approximate the size of the building (since most buildings are shaped in the form of a cube). Then the center of each small cube can be determined and given a coordinate location (see Figure 35b). The second step is to overlay this three-dimensional cube structure over the building and allocate crimes to the center of the cubes within which they occur (see Figure 35c). This method facilitates the computation of distances between crimes, using either direct line or Manhattan distances since each center has an X, Y, and Z coordinate.

A criticism of this method is that there will be a majority of null set cubes within which a crime will never be plotted. This is due to the fact that a crime will never occur on the ceiling. However, exactly where to plot it below the ceiling is open to interpretation. By convention, crimes are generally plotted on the floor below where they occur. But there is no reason not to plot them a cube or two above the floor if an item is stolen from a desk top, for example. The important point is to maintain consistency. Therefore, crimes are most likely to be plotted in cubes on the floor and in the middle of offices regardless of the exact location. Again, this leaves many cubes that will never be used if they are constructed small enough to provide accurate locations within the building.

Each method has strengths and weaknesses. Perhaps a refined or different method will be developed since this is a relatively uncharted approach to environmental criminology and crime analysis. Techniques used by anthropologists to map

Figure 31: Identifying a Cluster of Crime within a Building

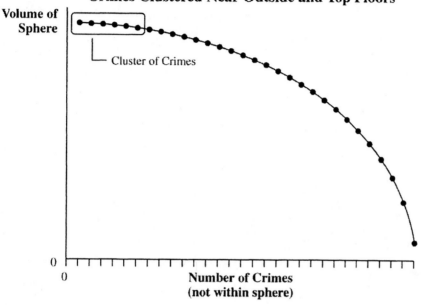

Crimes Clustered Near Outside and Top Floors

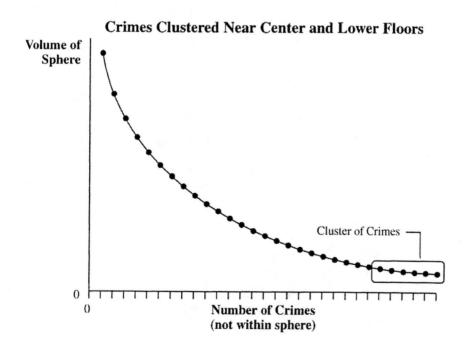

Crimes Clustered Near Center and Lower Floors

the location of artifacts in a dig may be applicable. However, since the location of artifacts is continuous rather than discrete in three dimensions, such techniques require modification. In artifact location, all possible locations in three dimensions may be used; in crime research, incidents are restricted to discrete locations.

Figure 32: Three-Dimensional Hot-Spot Analysis:
Method 1 – Step 1

Step 1. Sphere encompassing entire building

$$4/3\pi\ r^3$$

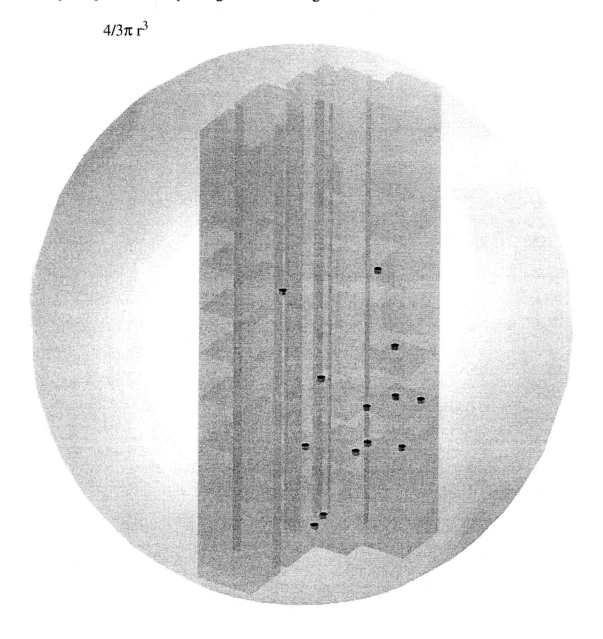

Figure 33: Three-Dimensional Hot-Spot Analysis:
Method 1 – Step 2

Step 2. Sphere encompassing crimes within building

Volume of sphere encompassing all
crime / volume of sphere
encompassing building

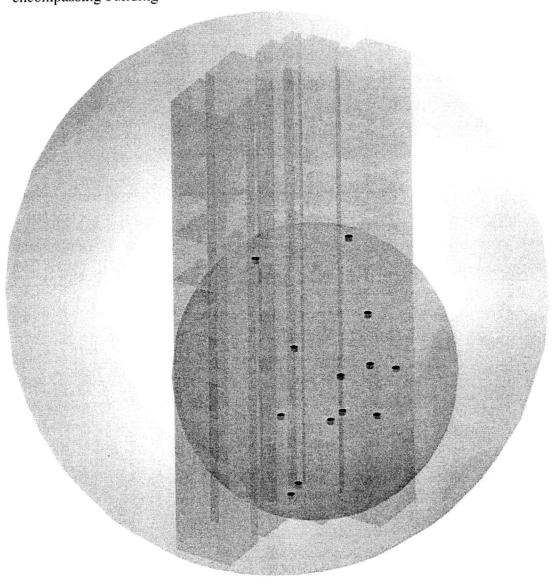

Figure 34: Three-Dimensional Hot-Spot Analysis:
Method 1 – Step 3

Step 3. Sphere encompassing 75 percent of crimes within building

Volume of sphere encompassing 75 percent of
all crime / volume of sphere
encompassing all crime
within building

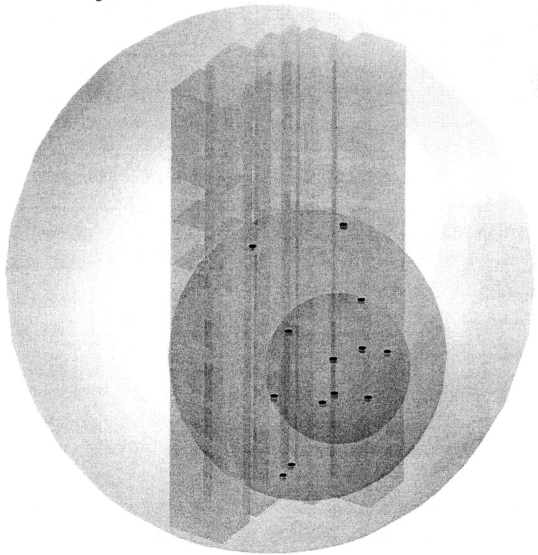

Figure 35: Cube Structure, Cube Overlay

A. Structure containing small cubes

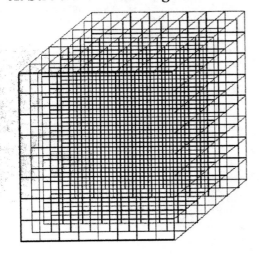

B. Centroid located in each cube

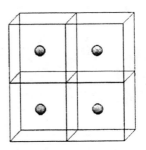

C. Overlay structure over building

REFERENCES

APBnews.com (1999). "College Community Crime." APBnews.com/resource center/datacenter/crimecheck/campus.

Bausell, C., B. Bausell and D. Siegel (1991). *The Links among Drugs, Alcohol, and Campus Crime.* Towson, MD: Campus Violence Prevention Center, Towson State University.

Beavon, D.J., P.L. Brantingham and P.J. Brantingham (1994). "The Influence of Street Networks on the Patterning of Property Offenses." In: R.V. Clarke (ed.), *Crime Prevention Studies*, vol. 2. Monsey, NY: Criminal Justice Press.

Block, C.R. (1994). "STAC Hot Spot Areas: A Statistical Tool for Law Enforcement Decisions." In: C.R. Block, M. Dabdoub and S. Fegly (eds.), *Crime Analysis Through Computer Mapping.* Washington, DC: Police Executive Research Forum.

Bordner, D.C. and D.M. Petersen (1983). *Campus Policing: The Nature of University Police Work.* New York, NY: University Press of America.

Boyer, E.L. (1990). *Campus Life in Search of Community.* Princeton, NJ: Carnegie Foundation.

Brantingham, P.L. and P.J. Brantingham (1995). "Crime and Fear of Crime at a Canadian University." In: B.S. Fisher and J.J. Sloan III (eds.), *Campus Crime: Legal, Social, and Policy Perspectives.* Springfield, IL: Charles C Thomas.

—— and P.J. Brantingham (1984). *Patterns in Crime.* New York, NY: Macmillan.

—— P.J. Brantingham and J. Seagrave (1995). "Crime and Fear of Crime at a Canadian University." In: B. Fisher and J Sloan (eds.), *Campus Crime: Legal, Social, and Policy Perspectives.* Springfield, IL: Charles C Thomas.

Bromley, M.L. (1999). "Community College Crime: An Exploratory Review." *Journal of Security Administration* 22(2):11-21.

—— (1995). "Securing the Campus: Political and Economic Factors Affecting Decision Makers." In B. Fisher and J. Sloan III (eds.), *Campus Crime: Legal, Social, and Policy Perspectives.* Springfield, IL: Charles C Thomas.

—— (1992). "Campus and Community Crime Rate Comparisons: A Statewide Study." *Journal of Security Administration* 15(2):49-64.

—— and L. Territo (1990). *College Crime Prevention and Personal Safety Awareness.* Springfield, IL: Charles C Thomas.

Brubacher, J.S. and W. Rudy (1976). *Higher Education in Transition* (3rd ed.). New York, NY: Harper and Row.

Capone, D. and W. Nichols (1976). "Urban Structure and Criminal Mobility." *American Behavioral Scientist* 20:199-213.

Chronicle of Higher Education (1999). Washington, DC: May 28. http://chronicle.com/ free/v45i38/stats/alihtm.

Clarke, R.V. (1992). *Situational Crime Prevention*. New York, NY: Harrow and Heston.

—— (1988). "Guest Editor's Introduction to the Special Issue on Situational Crime Prevention." *Journal of Security Administration* 11(2):4-6.

—— (1983). "Situational Crime Prevention: Its Theoretical Basis and Practical Scope." In: M. Tonry and N. Morris (eds.), *Crime and Justice: An Annual Review Of Research,* vol. 4. Chicago, IL: University of Chicago Press.

—— and P.M. Mayhew (1980). *Designing Out Crime*. London: Her Majesty's Stationery Office.

Clontz, K. and C.R. Jeffery (1992). "The Extent of Personal Crime on the Florida State University Main Campus: A Preliminary Report." Paper presented to the Academy of Criminal Justice Sciences annual meeting, Pittsburgh (March).

Cohen, L.E. and M. Felson (1979). "Social Change and Crime Rate Trends: A Routing Activity Approach." *American Sociological Review* 44:588-605.

Cornish, D.B. and R.V. Clarke (1986). *The Reasoning Criminal.* New York, NY: Springer-Verlag.

Dixon v. the Alabama Board of Education (1961). 294F.2d 150 (5th Cir. 1961), Cert. Denied, 368 U.S. 930.

Donnell v. California Western School of Law (1988). 200 Cal. JApp. 3d 715,246 Cal Rptr. 199 (4 Dist. 1988).

Felson, M.. (1986). "Predicting Crime Potential at any Point on the City Map." In: R. Figlio, S. Hakim and G. Rengert (eds.), *Metropolitan Crime Patterns*. Monsey, NY: Criminal Justice Press.

Fernandez, A. and A. Lizotte (1995). "An Analysis of the Relationship Between Campus Crime and Community Crime." In: B. Fisher and J. Sloan III (eds.), *Campus Crime: Legal, Social and Policy Perspectives*. Springfield, IL: Charles C Thomas.

Fisher, B. (1998). "Reducing Crime and Fear of Victimization on College and University Campuses, with Implications for Business and Industrial Parks." In: M. Felson and R. Preiser (eds.), *Crime Prevention Through Real Estate Management and Development*. Washington, DC: Urban Land Institute.

—— (1995). "Crime and Fear on Campus." *Annals of the American Academy of Political and Social Science* (May):85-101.

—— J. Sloan, F. Cullen and C. Lu (1998). "Crime in the Ivory Tower: The Level and Sources of Student Victimization." *Criminology* 36(3):671-710.

—— J. Sloan and D. Wilkins (1995). "Fear of Crime and Perceived Risk of Victimization on an Urban University Campus: A Test of Multiple Models." In: B. Fisher and J. Sloan III (eds.), *Campus Crime: Legal, Social, and Policy Perspectives*. Springfield, IL: Charles C Thomas.

—— and J. Sloan III (1993). "University Response to the Campus Security Act of 1990: Evaluating Programs Designed to Reduce Campus Crime." *Journal of Security Administration* 15(1):67-79.

—— and J. Nasar (1992). "Students' Fear of Crime and Its Relation to Physical Features of the Campus." *Journal of Security Administration* 15(2):65-75.

Fox, J. and D. Hellman (1985). "Location and Other Correlates of Campus Crime." *Journal of Criminal Justice* 13(4):429-444.

Goldstein, H. (1990). *Problem-Oriented Policing*. New York, NY: McGraw Hill.

Griffaton, M.C. (1995). "State-Level Initiatives and Campus Crime." In: B. Fisher and J. Sloan III (eds.), *Campus Crime: Legal, Social, and Policy Perspectives*. Springfield, IL: Charles C Thomas.

Hakim, S. and G. Rengert (1981). *Crime Spillover*. Beverly Hills, CA: Sage.

Harries, K. (1999). *Mapping Crime: Principles and Practice*. Washington, DC: Crime Mapping Research Center, U.S. National Institute of Justice.

Henderson, K. (1999). Unpublished personal communication, March 3.

Herbert, S. (1997). *Policing Space: Territoriality and the Los Angeles Police Department*. Minneapolis, MN: University of Minnesota Press.

Hoffman, A. (1971). *Steal This Book*. New York, NY: Grove Press.

—— (1970). *Revolution for the Hell of It*. New York, NY: Pocket Books.

Holtzman, H. (1997). Unpublished personal communication, July 8.

Kalette, D. (1990). "Violent Crime No Stranger on Campuses." *USA Today*, September 14, p.6A.

Kalstein, D. (1999). "Campus Crime Cover-up?" *Campus: America's Student Newspaper* 8(2) 1997:3-5.

Karp, H. (2001). "How Safe is Your Kid at College?" *Readers Digest* (April):82-89.

Leary, T. (1990). *The Politics of Ecstasy*. Berkeley, CA: Ronior Publications.

LeBeau, J. (1995). "The Temporal Ecology of Calls for Police Services." In: C.R. Block, M. Dabdoub, and S. Fregly (eds.), *Crime Analysis Through Computer Mapping*. Washington, DC: Police Executive Research Forum.

Letham, G. (2000). "College Crime Risk Mapping." *Spatial News*, November 12, p.1. http://www.Spatialnews.geocomm.com.

Lizotte, A.J. and A. Fernandez (1993). *Trends and Correlates of Campus Crime: A General Report.* Albany, NY: Consortium of Higher Education Campus Crime Research.

Mansour, N. and J. Sloan III (1992). "Campus Crime and Campus Communities: Theoretical And Empirical Linkages." Paper presented to the Academy of Criminal Justice Sciences annual meeting, Pittsburgh (March).

Matza, M. (1998). "A Focus for the Penn Crime Debate." *Philadelphia Inquirer,* Metro Section, April 1, p.1.

McConnell, E. (1996). "Students' Fear of Crime on a Southern University Campus." Paper presented to the Academy of Criminal Justice Sciences annual meeting, Las Vegas, Nevada (March).

McIver, J. (1981). "Criminal Mobility: A Review of Empirical Studies." In: S. Hakim and G. Rengert (eds.), *Crime Spillover.* Beverly Hills, CA: Sage.

McPheters, L. (1978). "Econometric Analysis of Factors Influencing Crime on the Campus." *Journal of Criminal Justice* 6(1):47-51.

Miller, J.L. and M.J. Pan (1987). "Student Perceptions of Campus Police: The Effects of Personal Characteristics and Police Contacts." *American Journal of Police* 6(1):27-44.

Morrill, R. (1965). "The Negro Ghetto: Problems and Alternatives." *Geographical Review* 55:339-361.

Newman, O. (1972). *Defensible Space: Crime Prevention Through Urban Design.* New York, NY: Macmillan.

Nichols, D. (1997). *Creating a Safe Campus: A Guide For College and University Administrators.* Springfield, IL: Charles C Thomas.

—— (1987). *The Administration of Public Safety in Higher Education.* Springfield, IL: Charles C Thomas.

Odland, J. (1988). *Spatial Autocorrelation.* London, UK: Sage.

Otey, A. (2000). "Will The Clery Act Amendments to the Higher Education Act Affect Student Safety?" http://www.matrix-magazine.com/print.php?...les/features/sidebar/cleryadct.html&title=.

Peak, K.J. (1995). "The Professionalization of Campus Law Enforcement: Comparing Campus and Municipal Law Enforcement Agencies." In: B.S. Fisher and J.J. Sloan III (eds.), *Campus Crime: Legal, Social, and Policy Perspectives.* Springfield, IL: Charles C Thomas.

Pearson, F.S. and J. Toby (1991). "Fear of School-Related Predatory Crime." *Sociology and Social Research* 75(3):117-119.

Peterson v. San Francisco Community College District (1984). 685 P. 2d 1193 (Cal. 1984).

Pettiway, L. (1982). "The Mobility of Robbery and Burglary Offenders: Ghetto and Non-Ghetto Spaces." *Urban Affairs Quarterly* 18(2):255-270.

Rand, G. and N. Levine (1989). "Assessing Crime and Incidents in University Residence Halls: An Ecological Approach." Los Angeles, CA: University of California at Los Angeles, mimeo.

Raper, J.F. and B. Kelk (1991). "Three-Dimensional GIS." In: D.J. Maguire, M.F. Goodchild and D. Rhind (eds.), *Geographical Information Systems: Principles and Applications.* New York, NY: John Wiley.

Rengert, G. (1997). "Auto Theft in Central Philadelphia." In: R. Homel (ed.), *Crime Prevention Studies*, vol. 7. Monsey, NY: Criminal Justice Press.

—— (1996). *The Geography of Illegal Drugs.* Boulder, CO: Westview Press.

—— and J. Wasilchick (2000). *Suburban Burglary: A Tale of Two Suburbs.* Springfield, IL: Charles C Thomas.

—— and J. Wasilchick (1985). *Suburban Burglary: A Time and a Place For Everything.* Springfield, IL: Charles C Thomas.

Roach, C. (2000a). "The Jeanne Clery Disclosure of Campus Security Policy and Campus Crime Statistics Act." *Matrix Unbound,* November 11. http://www.matrix-magazine.com.

—— (2000b). "Drawing a Bead on Campus Crime." *Matrix Unbound.* November 11. http://www.matrix-magazine.com.

Rossmo, K. (1995). "Overview: Multivariate Spatial Profiles as a Tool in Crime Investigation." In: C.R. Block, M. Dabdoub and S. Fregly (eds.), *Crime Analysis Through Computer Mapping.* Washington, DC: Police Executive Research Forum.

Seng, M. and N. Koehler (1993). "The Crime Awareness and Campus Security Act: A Critical Analysis." *Journal of Crime and Justice* 16(1):97-110.

Shaw, C. and H. McKay (1969). *Juvenile Delinquency In Urban Areas.* Chicago, IL: University of Chicago Press.

Sherman, L.W. and D. Weisburd (1995). "General Deterrent Effects of Police Patrol in Crime 'Hot Spots': A Randomized, Controlled Trial." *Justice Quarterly* 12:625-648.

Sherrill, J. and D. Siegel (eds.) (1989). *Responding to Violence on Campus.* San Francisco, CA: Jossey-Bass.

Sides, E. (1983) "Policing the Campus: Responsibilities of a University Police Department." *The Police Chief* 50(November):69-70.

Siegel, D. and C. Raymond (1992). "An Ecological Approach to Violent Crime on Campus." *Journal of Security Administration* 15(2):19-29.

Sloan, J. III (1994). "The Correlates of Campus Crime: An Analysis of Reported Crimes on College and University Campuses." *Journal of Criminal Justice* 22:51-61.

—— (1992a). "Campus Crime and Campus Communities." *Journal of Security Administration* 15(2):31-49.

—— (1992b). "The Modern Campus Police: An Analysis of their Evolution, Structure, and Function." *American Journal of Police* 11(1):85-104.

—— and B. Fisher (1994). "Providing More than a Glimpse of the Extent of Crime on Campuses." *The Chronicle of Higher Education* XL(26) (March 2), p.B3.

Smith, M.C. (1995). "Vexatious Victims of Campus Crime." In: B. Fisher and J. Sloan III (eds.), *Campus Crime: Legal, Social, and Policy Perspectives*. Springfield, IL: Charles C Thomas.

—— (1989). "The Ancestry of Campus Violence." In: J. Sherrill and D. Siegel (eds.), *Responding to Violence on Campus*. San Francisco, CA: Jossey-Bass.

—— and M.D. Smith (1990). *Wide Awake: A Guide to Safe Campus Living in the 90's*. Princeton, NJ: Peterson's Guides.

Smith, W., S. Frazee and E. Davison (2000). "Furthering the Integration of Routine Activity and Social Disorganization Theories: Small Units of Analysis and the Study of Street Robbery as a Diffusion Process." *Criminology* 38(2):489-524.

Stormer, D.E. and D.T. Senarath (1992). "The Truth About Campus Crime: An Analysis of Campus Crime Reports for Three Years in Pennsylvania." *The Campus Law Enforcement Journal* 22(4):28-32.

"Student Right-To-Know and Campus Security Act of 1990 (1990)." Public Law No. 101-542 (1990); amended by Public Law No. 102-26, Sec. 10(e) (1991); 20 U.S.C. 1092(f).

Surette, R. (1992). *Media, Crime and Criminal Justice*. Pacific Grove, CA: Brooks-Cole.

Turner, S. (1969). "Delinquency and Distance." In: T. Sellin and M. Wolfgang (eds.), *Delinquency: Selected Studies*. New York, NY: John Wiley.

United States Department of Education, Office of Postsecondary Education, Policy, Planning and Evaluation (2001). *The Incidence of Crime on the Campuses of U.S. Postsecondary Education Institutions*. Washington, DC.

United States Department of Education (1991). *Digest of Education Statistics*. Washington, DC.

United States Federal Bureau of Investigation (yearly). *Uniform Crime Reports*. Washington, DC: U.S. Department of Justice.

White, R.C. (1932). "The Relationship of Felonies to Environmental Factors in Indianapolis." *Social Forces* 10(4):498-509.

Wilkins, D.L. (1996). "The Spatial and Temporal Distribution of Crime on a University Campus: A 'Hot Spots' Analysis." A thesis submitted to the Department of Justice Sciences, the University of Alabama at Birmingham.

Zahm, D. and D. Perrin (1992). "Safe for Study: Designing the Campus Environment." *Journal of Security Administration* 15:77-99.